WEB QUEST

by

GRACE CAREY

The true story of a black quest across the East Anglian countryside.

Wyrd Books

Published in 1996 by Wyrd Books
c/o Masefield Road Post Office
Masefield Road
Braintree
Essex
CM7 1AA

British Library Cataloguing Publication Data
ISBN 0 9528321 0 0

Photography by Grace Carey
Printed and bound by Circle Services, Southend.

Front cover origination by Grace Carey and Richard Carey

TO ANNE MOWLING FOR SHARING THE BENEFIT OF HER TALENT

ACKNOWLEDGEMENTS

My sincere thanks must be offered to those without whom this book would not have been possible; Duncan Bittle, my boyfriend, for his encouragement and advice. Richard Ward for being our reluctant leader. Jason Cormick, Brian Mowling, Jason Digby and Cally Peacock for being part of the gang. Richard Carey, my brother for helping me into print. Peter and Shirley Carey, my father and mother, for their support and the use of their computer. Andrew Collins for teaching us the basics. Last but not least, all my friends who have offered moral support.

Extra thanks must also go the proof readers; Richard Ward, Anne Mowling, John Bonwick, Ronnie Everet and Geoff Webb.

CONTENTS

INTRODUCTION

This is a tale of psychic questing. A means of solving hidden mysteries left imprinted on the energies of the land and finding concealed artifacts by the power of the mind.

A quest may begin in many ways, often with a psychic 'tuning in' to a site and sensing a message. This may happen intentionally or perhaps spontaneously. The information received could be by a vision or communicating with a site guardian figure (a thought-form left behind from the past to watch over and spiritually care for the site). This material may lead to questions and a quest will have begun. Alternatively a quest may be started by another means, a dream perhaps, but for the purposes of this book I shall deal with how we came upon the web.

Those of us involved all met through Earthquest, an earth mysteries, questing, research etc. group run by Andrew Collins in Leigh-on-sea. We have since, as a group of friends, been going out into the countryside and putting the theory into practice. Anne Mowling is the most prominent psychic of our group to whom we owe most of the information for this quest. The other members, who provide the research, map work, local knowledge etc. include Richard Ward, Jason Cormick (Big Jason), Jason Digby (Jason D) and his girlfriend Cally Peacock, Duncan Bittle and myself.

It was a quest stumbled upon quite by accident, but was to lead us to 13 sites across Essex, Suffolk and Hertfordshire. We suspected we were following the trail of a coven working on linking up a network of sites. At best we felt they were selfish in their magic and at worst corrupt, harmful and dangerous. Our quest was to try and weaken their power and redress the balance of the energies of the land.

It was what is known as a black quest. This is when you're dealing with dark influences left behind by an individual or group of people who are practising a dubious form of magic. This kind of questing can make psychics quite ill both physically and mentally, so we had to insure we were sufficiently psychically protected. We only have our own opinion of what is healthy or harmful magic to go on but we all felt that the trail being left behind by this particular group we were following was not in harmony with the site's natural energies and therefore must be detrimental for the land.

This story is a factual account of a true sequence of events. Things don't always go as planned in questing and so hence this is a 'warts and all' account of our story. Please forgive the parts where we get lost or fail to produce tangible results, but this is a hazard of the pursuit of questing. Psychics aren't infallible and real life gets in the way all too often. Having said that, this was a very successful and complete quest. We achieved many good results, learnt along the way and had an exciting time.

Chapter One

THE QUEST BEGINS

Richard Ward, Anne Mowling and Jason Cormick set out one evening in late July 1994 for East Hanningfield; they were looking for the site of the old church. Richard knew of an original site and was curious as to where it was as no indication of it was marked on the map. In a conversation had at an Earthquest meeting it was revealed that Jason knew the location of the site so the outing was arranged.

The church site is situated down a network of country lanes well away from the present day village, near a large hall. The original church was behind this hall and was gutted by fire on 30 December, 1883. The new church in the village was built in 1885. They drove down the long straight lane (obviously enough, once you know where it is, called Old Church Road) enjoying the beautiful summers evening. Having parked the car on the grass verge they walked the short distance along the footpath to the copse of trees. The scene which greeted them was like that from an old horror film. The tombs stood gaping, cracked open by tree roots and grave stones leaned at rakish angles from behind bushes and brambles. The whole site, a place which was once holy ground was gradually being claimed back by nature. They took a short walk around marvelling at how a graveyard could be so forgotten and left to rot, before settling down in a far corner to conduct a meditation. As they opened their minds to the influences at the site, Anne instantly felt agitated. She was aware something was wrong, that somehow the site had been ritually abused. Neither the fine weather, country air or picturesque setting could lessen the feeling. She got flashes in her mind of a group and imagery of the suit of Spades in a pack of cards. More than anything though she could sense there was an imbalance at the woodland which was creating a disharmony in the atmosphere.

Breaking off from the meditation she suddenly felt drawn to a particular headstone nearby. Instinctively she knew that an object concealed there was at the root of the trouble. She hurriedly called to Richard to look. "It's here, a sword or something buried." Richard parted the long grass and there with the tip pushed into the ground at the base of the headstone was a sword-shaped letter opener. Amazing confirmation of Anne's considerable psychic talents.

They felt someone had probably left the knife as a 'fixing marker':- An object which has been charged with magical energy or had a spell of some sort imbued into it by a ritual or visualisation. This then seeps out into the land and atmosphere of a site corrupting the energies. Not all fixing markers are harmful, some can enhance or protect, but the feeling was that this knife had been left by someone for some purpose which had not been in harmony with the site itself. This had led to the natural energy balance at the site being upset and had

The headstone in East Hanningfield's disused churchyard where Anne sensed the source of the disturbance.

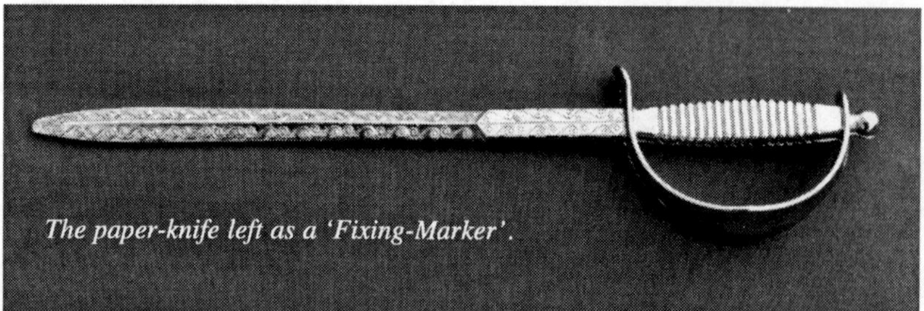

The paper-knife left as a 'Fixing-Marker'.

dramatically changed the atmosphere for the worst.

"It feels hot." Richard exclaimed having retrieved the knife, throwing it from one hand to the other to avoid contact with it for too long. "We've got to get it to some water to clean it." He offered the artefact for the others to look at. An offer declined by Anne as she could feel that holding the offending article would make her ill.

"There's a brook down by where we left the cars," remembered Jason. So they hastily left to go and douse the paper-knife in the stream. Richard felt a real urgency to get the knife washed. It felt as if it was pulsing but the water would help to cleanse the object and nullify this effect of the magic from it.

As they returned to the cars they were approached by a woman. "What are you doing here? This is private property," she stated haughtily.

"Oh sorry, we didn't know, there's no sign. We'd just parked here to have a walk along the footpath," Anne explained hastily hoping the woman would hurry on her way.

After confirming they were just leaving and wouldn't park there again the lady returned to her house. Richard plunged the knife into the brook with a look of relief spreading across his face. Once cleaned he carefully examined the artefact; it was about 7 inches long, gold in colour and semi-ornate.

This find posed many questions. Who had left such a magically charged item in these woods and why? Were there more similar desecration at other sites?

With most of its magical energy now cleansed from it, Anne agreed to handle the object to psychometrise it. She felt the woods had been visited by a group of 13 people, the number usually associated with a witches coven. Her psychic impressions told her that they were laying out a network of sites in the form of a spider's web over the landscape. Anne drew a sketch map of the web and East Hanningfield fell in the most south-easterly corner. There were 12 points around the outside and 1 in the centre, 13 points in all. She felt the group were using the imagery of the suit of spades in a pack of cards for their magic. She could see the woman who called herself the Queen of Spades as if she were still there. Anne described her as a dark haired woman with a centre parting and an overbite to her mouth. This 'Queen of Spades' was laying the artifacts and her Knave, the 'Jack of Spades' was collecting them back up after they had served their purpose. Anne thought this knife had been placed there for no more than a couple of weeks. Knowing from her information that there were more sites which had been similarly desecrated, she could gain a few clues about the next point on the web they had visited if moving in an anti-clockwise direction. It was a town or village with a water-mill, a pub called 'The Swan' and a church. This place would probably be in a roughly north-easterly direction from East Hanningfield.

They left the site with a quest started, an artefact had been retrieved and clues to the next site had been gained. With the harmful object removed East Hanningfield old churchyard could start to heal itself and restore its natural balance.

CHAPTER TWO

ON THE TRAIL

We all heard the story of what happened at East Hanningfield at the following Earthquest meeting of Monday 1 August. Everyone put forward suggestions as to the next site, the place with a water-mill, a pub called 'The Swan' and a church. Of all the places mentioned only one seemed to have all the criteria. Jason had found out from a workmate that there was a water-mill at Hatfield Peverel, a place just off the A12 between Chelmsford and Witham, to the north-north-east of East Hanningfiled. There is also a pub called The Swan and a large church set in a secluded churchyard to the south of the village. It seemed the only place that fitted so Anne, Richard, Jason and my boyfriend, Duncan and I arranged to go and check it out on the following Wednesday.

We congregated outside Jason's house in Danbury, and as Duncan and I had missed the first site it was decided that a return visit to East Hanningfield was in order. This would serve as a recap on the story so far for our benefit and also to see if the group had returned and placed another artefact.

Anne's impressions on this second visit were that the group had not returned but were fully aware of our interference and the removal of their fixing marker. During a meditation she also picked up this time on a name. "Coga... something", Anne started to say, which the rest of us who come from further north in the county could fill in to be Coggeshall. A place with a reputation for witchcraft. She also stressed she'd seen a ruin in her vision. This gave us more food for future thought.

Having decided the site had remained clean we set about thinking where to head for next. Hatfield Peverel would definitely be a point of call, as would Coggeshall but as yet we had no idea of the scale to which the

Queen and her group were working. Could there possibly be other sites closer? We checked the maps for any likely location along the way and found that not far away was a priory ruin in a field at Bicknacre, also near a pub called 'The Swan'. Richard knew of this place and of another psychic who had in the past described it as a 'time gateway'. This seemed as good a place to start as any, so as it was on the way we thought we would stop off to have a quick look.

Having found the right footpath we started across the cow fields, treading carefully as we went. The Augustinian priory ruins suddenly came into view one field over. They consists of a large archway and section of wall, making an impressive sight looming up in the middle of a meadow. Once we had arrived for a closer look we all commented that this was definitely a powerful place. It had probably been used many times for magical purposes but Anne felt it had not been visited by the Queen of Spades and her group. It had been well worth visiting nevertheless. Once back at the cars we journeyed on, cutting across country to Hatfield Peverel.

Dusk was just starting to fall by the time we pulled into the long driveway of this imposing church dedicated to St Andrew. We all went our separate ways and started to meander round the churchyard with its mass of graves and ancient trees. I wandered over to a large blackened tree stump, (probably a casualty of the storm of 1987) and noticed drawn on it

The church of St Andrews, Hatfield Peverel, with the large blackened tree stump in the foreground.

in chalk was a large cross. This was clearly not natural and quite recent. The sight of this sent a shiver up my spine a left me feeling decidedly spooked. This was perhaps our first clue that we were on the right path.

We gathered round to conduct a meditation to find out if we were at the correct place and if so, was there an artefact left here which needed to be removed. Anne said the first positive yes, but we all felt the atmosphere was not as it should be as twilight was rapidly drawing closer to darkness. Anne could see a haze of light all around a group of trees near where the footpath to the church enters its grounds. This is her way of psychically seeing where an artefact may be hidden and she felt sure another knife had been left in the vicinity. She also felt that not all the group had been to this site. The artefact meant it could take only one person to complete their work.

We checked the ground for signs of something having been buried, and in the crevices on the tree trunks searching for anything out of place concealed there. However, in the fading light and with only one small torch with low batteries, we didn't stand much chance of finding anything. Having all blundered round for sometime we stopped to collect our thoughts. Bats flew up into the night sky overhead, setting out on their nightly foray for food, as we discussed the situation. Eventually we determined not to be beaten and decided on a systematic approach. Starting at the tree which appeared most in line with the tree stump with the cross drawn on it, and was closest to the path, we renewed our search.

After only a couple of minutes Richard exclaimed he had found something. We all hurried to gather round. As Anne had correctly said, it was a knife, hidden amongst some of the suckers growing from the trunk. It was about 6 inches long, had a pava shell handle and a curved blade like that of a scimitar.

The small knife retrieved from the base of a tree in Hatfield Peverel churchyard.

This had the same 'pulsey' feeling to it, although it was not hot like the first artefact had been. Having each examined it (with the exception of Anne) we set off to try and find some water to cleanse it in. It was a graveyard, so we reasoned that there had to be a tap around somewhere for people to water flowers with. While we searched Richard repeatedly shook his hand to try and revive some life back into it. Like the paper knife, this new artefact had also made his hand go numb. Eventually, on a far wall there was the promised tap and Richard hurriedly plunged the knife into the stream of cold water until he felt most of the magical potency of the knife had been wash away. Elated at our success on this quest, having removed two artifacts and cleaned up two desecrated sites we returned to the cars.

What to do next was the question. Should we all head home or carry on? We were already fairly sure that the next site was Coggeshall. The distance on the map between East Hanningfield and Hatfield Peverel was much the same as that between Hatfield Peverel and Coggeshall and the general direction compared to Anne's sketch seemed correct. It therefore seemed reasonable to presume Anne's information was correct. It should perhaps be pointed out that Anne has absolutely no sense of direction whatsoever, so there could be no way that she guessed likely sites in her mind as we went along. While we were on a roll and eager, we decided to continue on and see what Coggeshall held in store for us.

We knew of some abbey ruins in Coggeshall and from the information which Anne had received earlier it seemed an apt site to begin the next stage of our search. None of us had ever been to these remains, so we found the small track which they were marked next to on the map and driving slowly we kept our eyes peeled for the promised ruins. The map however, was vague and showed no exact spot. We parked the cars and shining our feeble torch (bring better torches next time, we all noted) across the field we tried to make out any shape which may suggest a ruin silhouetted against the sky but the darkness had beaten us. We returned once again to the cars which we had left near a small chapel and just in passing, it was mentioned by all that it had a strange feel to it. The subject then changed as we all said our goodbyes and arranged to return in the daylight to continue our quest.

* * * * * * *

Later, on being able to check out the meaning of some of the imagery which Anne had received, it looked like this group were (in our opinion) definitely up to no good. They had chosen to use imagery from a pack of playing cards, rather than the Tarot cards from which the original concept comes. Playing cards are steeped in magical tradition; the 52 cards in a pack represent the 52 weeks of the year, the 13 cards in each suit are the 13 lunar months and the 4 suits represent the elements, dimension, winds, seasons, worlds, etc. The picture cards of the King, Queen and Knave originate from the spiritual triad of the father figure or spirit, the mother figure or soul and the ego or energies.

The Spades which they had chosen as their symbols were very dark and heavy in aspect. Both black suits represent the cold seasons and the powers of darkness. The Spades particularly are symbolic of death and in divination they warn of danger ahead in all manner of forms, such as misfortune, loss, suffering, treachery and failure. The Queen particularly is symbolic of an unscrupulous dark haired woman and related to war, while the knave is her acquaintance and messenger.

The knife is a symbol very much associated, as may be expected, with sacrifice, death, severance and vengeance. The blade imagery can also bring us back to the tarot as the Swords suit in the tarot is what has now become the Spades in playing cards.

The web itself is now a symbol of fear to mankind. Many people have the classic fear of spiders, arachnophobia and the web which is always to be found in dark untouched corners is representative of that fear. However, in ancient times the spider was a revered and respected creature, seen as the weaver of destiny, the web of wyrd. Also an aspect of the lunar goddess, the great mother. The web depicts the cycles of life and death, creation and destruction with its similarity to the wheel of existence. There is birth on the edge of the web with its ever increasing circles but death lurks at the centre.

The number 13 is also representative of life and death. The group, we believed to have 13 members and the web which Anne had described had 13 points. It seemed there was a balance in the imagery in some parts of this unfolding scene, but in others the death aspect far outweighed the life.

I pondered on what exactly this group may be up to, it all seemed very negative and the atmosphere they had left behind at both places was, we felt, far from favourable. However, from the clues we had so far it was hopeless to try and guess at the exact purposes of their errant magic and the methods or rituals they were employing to carry out these desecrations.

Chapter Three

A CONCEALED PATH AHEAD

We all met next on Monday 8 August, again by the little chapel of St Nicholas in Coggeshall. Maps out we set off down the track looking for the ruins.

Anne felt we were definitely in the right area but look as hard as we might we could see no sign of any ruins across the fields. We were all gathered round the maps busy looking lost when a lady approached us to see what we were doing. We explained that we were interested in historical buildings and were looking for the abbey remains. "You've just walked past them, we live in them," she said, as we all looked back to the beautiful house, each of us wondering why we hadn't realised that it bore a great similarity to abbey buildings.

After chatting a while she offered to show us the barn and cloisters. They were beautiful buildings which we were glad to see. She told us that the cloisters and the chapel were made of early medieval bricks, possibly the oldest in England and the Abbey was built in 1140 and the chapel around 1200, both by Cistercian monks. All very interesting but obviously as this was a private residence, this could not have been the site used by the coven. Having taken some pictures we said thank you and goodbye and wandered back up the track.

We seemed to have lost our thread, but thought we'd have a look at the chapel near by, maybe they'd used that instead, as like us, on finding the abbey remains lived in, they would also choose the next best and nearest site. Once at the chapel we had soon completed our initial perusal of the grounds. Having settled ourselves down on the concrete path, we conducted a meditation and tried to locate in our minds where exactly the group would have visited; here or somewhere else. Anne and Jason both felt we were at the correct place, so we all set about looking in the long grass around the base of the walls, peering into the nooks in the stonework and even fishing about in a nearby old horse trough. After sometime of unsuccessful searching we paused for thought.

"So what do you think then Anne?" Richard questioned. "I don't know. It's around the door I think. I can see a small cross this time but I don't know what it's made out of," Anne replied. The cross is of course the most obvious symbol of the Christian religion, so were they now mocking this religion by desecrating not only its hallowed ground but also its imagery? Again we searched but once again drew a blank. Anne was sure an artefact had been there but there was certainly nothing in evidence now. We decided if they knew of our presence on their trail then maybe they would leave artifacts only for the minimum length of time necessary for their desired affect and then remove them. If so, then perhaps we had missed out on finding something the first time we were there.

With the artefact gone it was now time to turn our minds to the next

St Nicholas' Chapel, Coggeshall. Was this the third site on the web?

site they had used (and abused). Anne felt blocked during this meditation and none of the rest of us gained any clues. It seemed that either they had put up a psychic wall to block us out or that the energies of the chapel where the artefact had rested were affecting Anne in some adverse way. During the meditation we visualised the area being cleansed. This consisted of picturing clean white light both covering and penetrating the whole locality and purging any taint left by the artefact.

We decided to move on to the main church of St Peter's in Coggeshall to see if being away from the chapel would help any. Unfortunately once there Anne still couldn't clear her mind. It was definitely a psychic wall put up around the location of the next site. We would have to do a meditation to try and break this wall down. This blocking also re-affirmed Anne's suspicion that our opposing group knew of our presence on their trail.

Having found a quiet corner of the churchyard, we sat down on a group of box tombs (we were sure the occupants wouldn't mind) and fidgeted to get comfortable before we all began to relax our minds. Richard began to speak after a few moments and talk us through the meditation. "See a wall in front of you, know that this is the wall Anne is seeing concealing the next site..... See a line of energy run from you towards the wall, see it joining with everyone else's and know this will be powerful enough to break a hole in the wall for us to see through." As we all saw this imagery we pictured a hole beginning to appear and break down the wall around it. Brick by brick we forced this breach larger until the opening was big enough for a clear view through. Once this was done we knew that Anne, with her perceptive powers, would be able to see through and give us the clues we needed.

It worked! With her head bowed still in meditation she described what she could see. "There's a large box-like building on a large mound that's supposed to be surrounded by water but isn't."

"Castle Hedingham", Richard, Jason, Duncan and myself all chorused, recognising this description. We had our fourth site.

It was still early enough not to call it a day yet, so off we set again. This time in a slightly different direction. We were now heading to the north-north-west.

Castle Hedingham, from which the village takes its name, is a large keep set on a prominence overlooking the Colne valley. It is 100 feet high and the walls are 11 feet thick. This impressive feat of construction was commissioned by Aubrey de Vere, one of the powerful Earls of Oxford in 1140. The 4 span bridge over the moat was built in the fifteenth century. Richard and Duncan had both visited it before so we found it quickly and easily.

The castle was closed by now, so having parked the cars on the road we tip-toed quietly passed the gatehouse and made our way up towards the trees on the summit of the large mound. Darkness had fallen and we all skulked around guiltily in the shadows. We were trying to work out how to get up to the castle without going passed the main house which had light glaring out from it and which was situated right next to the bridge. There was nothing for it but to scramble up the steep bank of the moat. With us all slipping down as fast as we were getting up we must have made a ludicrous sight. With the help of Jason's walking stick being dangled down

The Keep of Castle Hedingham.

and a few tree roots we eventually all made it up. Turning our attention to the quest we tried to stop giggling under our breaths and get serious. Stepping out through the trees, the sight of the imposing Norman keep looming up at us looked creepy to say the least and soon wiped the smiles off our faces. We all hurried round to the opposite side of the castle so our torch light would not be seen from the house.

"Yeah, this is definitely what I saw," said Anne gazing up at the huge walls silhouetted against the clear night sky. She got the impression that this time it was another cross which they had left and she could see a glow across a section of wall near the back of the castle. By torch-light we once again set about a search, only to find that they were getting better at hiding them. With the knowledge of us on their tail they must be taking more care in concealing the artifacts. However we all felt they had been there and that once again the energies were unbalanced. Foiled by darkness again we returned to the cars and again arranged to return in the daylight.

The section of wall at the South-Westerly corner of the castle where Anne felt another fixing marker may have been hidden.

Chapter Four

THE CASTLE AND THE DWARF

On Wednesday 17 August, Richard, Anne, Jason, Duncan and I were joined by Jason Digby. We arrived at Castle Hedingham, despite our best efforts, once again after closing time. This meant skulking round the bushes again, so rather than going all the way up to the castle we lingered in the woods near the road to attune to the castle. Anne felt the artefact of the cross that she had sensed up at the castle the other night had now been removed but not she felt, by a member of their group. Possibly we thought it was found by a visitor to the castle. Whatever had happened to it Anne felt it was no longer there so we decided against returning to the keep and clambering up the bank again.

Instead we turned our attention to a meditation to clean up the castle and its grounds on a spiritual level, and to see if we could get any clues as to where to head for next. Having completed a breathing exercise to prepare for a meditation we all fell silent. The breathing exercise consisted of visualising the breathing in pure clean white light through your nose and breathing out dirty grey from your mouth. By this method you can relax by concentrating on your breathing and at the same time cleanse your body in preparation for going into a medative state. Once in this state we could all guide our minds to the issue in hand, to see if we could discover any more clues for the quest. After five minutes or so, when we had all opened our eyes, Anne told us that she got the feeling of an ecclesiastical building of some description, a priory or convent.

We returned to the cars to search the maps for a likely location. Quite a distinctive pattern of a spiders web was already forming with fairly uniform distances and angles between each site. All we had to do now was continue the pattern. It headed now into Suffolk and the most likely place to start looking seemed to be Clare with its wealth of possibilities. The distance was a little too short but we decided not to place too much sway on the map. If they were marking out a spiders web symbolically, it wouldn't necessarily need to be geographically accurate.

Clare had numerous feasible sites of an ancient or sacred nature. There are two priories, one still in use and the other ruined. The latter was part of a castle complex of which remnants, including a motte and bailey, are to be seen at various spots over the town. Further over to the north-eastern side of the town is an iron age camp, now in use as a recreation area and also a small ruined chapel was marked on the map. Clare also boasts a beautiful church in the centre of town which is on the site of another part of the castle.

Having first tried the ruined chapel (which we couldn't find) and the used priory, which was clearly not an option once we saw it, we went in search of the disused priory. Once again darkness had by now fallen and we aimlessly wandered along the riverbank and a disused railway line. In our evenings walk we passed by the motte and bailey and thought as we hadn't found the priory yet we'd check the castle first. The motte and bailey, which is the largest part of the remains, standing 53 feet high and has a section of the keep wall still standing on its summit. The castle is of Norman origin and at one time covered 20 acres.

With careful steps we wound our way along the narrow path around the small but steep, wooded hill. Everyone began to feel uneasy about this place. Walking along under the cover of the trees the darkness had become noticeably darker. Once at the top we gathered around the large section of wall and prepared to carry out a meditation. It seemed this wasn't necessary though, as Anne confirmed this was definitely the place they had used. We all very readily agreed with her as the atmosphere had put us all on edge. Anne sensed that more of the group, possibly all of them had come to this site.

Even though Anne had seen a religious building of some description and the castle was obviously not of that nature, we had still ended up at the correct place. Her clues had still got us here as the priory and castle were part of the same complex. It seemed that our not being able to find the priory, (which I've since found very easily in the daylight and from which you can actually see the mound of the motte) was perhaps meant to be.

Anne suddenly saw a flash at the base of the wall, her psychic signpost. So once again we all set about looking where the flash had happened to find if they had left another fixing marker.

After a time of looking Richard commented to Anne, "Do you sense any presences here?"

"Yes, didn't I say earlier, there's a black dwarf over there just behind Grace," she announced calmly. Richard confirmed that he could see it too and that it was not a nice cuddly variety of elemental. 'Oh great', I thought, as I moved forward, away from the trees and bushes which Anne and Richard indicated this dwarf was hidden amongst. The rest of us strained our eyes, peering into the darkness. We would have to take their word for it as our eyes lacked the vision and ability to really *see* the way in which Anne and Richard (to a lesser degree) were gifted.

Elementals are basically raw energy which has taken on or been given a form by our sub-conscious. Different types of elemental have certain elements with which they are generally associated, hence the name. Dwarfs are usually considered, along with gnomes, to be connected with the element of the earth and are often considered mischievous and childlike. They often appear black in appearance. This can be accredited to the nature of their work, that of smiths, with the soot from the forges coating them from head to toe. To find a dwarf on a large mound would not be unexpected due to the strong earth element of any hill. However, this particular little chap was clearly not your run-of-the-mill member of the wild folk going about his business, his intent seemed to be malicious.

By now we were all feeling decidedly uncomfortable or ill, so we

The wall on top of Clare Castle,
behind which Anne and Richard could see an elemental creature.

conducted a cleansing meditation by raising the cone of power (see Appendix) and seeing pure clean energy washing over the whole of the hill, penetrating deep into the earth and surrounding area. Having completed the visualisation we all commented on how it seemed to have had the opposite affect to that which we intended. Anne meanwhile was quite shaken, she had had the overwhelming urge to push Richard through a gap in the fence and down the steep slope. "I don't know how I managed to stop myself," she exclaimed. It appeared that the elemental had been influencing Anne to have this totally encompassing urge. Luckily for Richard she was strong enough to resist.

The dwarf was now gone but rather than a pleasant calm atmosphere it seemed more oppressive than ever. Somehow the cleaning energy we had put into the site had been warped and turned into the negative which we felt the coven were using. With us all feeling highly agitated by the atmosphere there we made our way back down the hill.

While hurrying down Jason D. (who was walking in front of Anne) stumbled and fell, twisting his leg. Jokingly we all suggested that Anne had pushed him. Our laughter raised the atmosphere a little and eased the nagging fear and trepidation we were all feeling. We had definitely experienced a very weird night, and were all glad to return to the safety and comfort of our own homes.

Looking back now at the pattern of what we've found it seems that at the very secluded sites where there is very little chance of the group being disturbed they have carried out a full ritual to set up a guardian thought-form instead of just leaving a fixing marker with their magic already contained in it. This dwarf it seemed was such a thought-form or trapped elemental and he seemed to emanate from the spot by the wall where Anne had seen the flash.

CHAPTER FIVE

THE SEAL

The quest was left for a week or so after this episode as Anne had been quite poorly after the previous encounter. We next arranged to meet on Sunday 28 August so we could hopefully find a couple of sites in the daylight. Richard, Jason D and Cally Peacock, Anne and her husband Brian all met at where Duncan and I live in Finchingfield. Over a cup of coffee Anne told us her thoughts on the clues to the next site. She could see a church with a square tower, a jagged shape in front of it and a curved driveway leading to it. It was all she could give us and although we would probably recognise it when we saw it, it wasn't much to go on. The map didn't offer many clues now either as we knew we would now be taking a turn to the west or north-west This widened our area to search considerably.

We began at Castle Camps church as Duncan and I knew there to be another motte and bailey castle there and the remains of a medieval village. It seemed to have the right criteria of an ancient sacred place. We walked around the churchyard and surrounding fields and soaked up the atmosphere. It was a beautiful sunny day and we were all laughing and joking, it felt really good there. It seemed clear to us all that this was not the place.

We went on to try Shudy Camps church which provided no further clues. We had the thought that perhaps if we could boost Anne's psychic energy level she could maybe provide us with some more clues. As we were nearby we opted to go and visit a place known as Bartlow hills, these large tumuli are the biggest burial mounds in Europe and are of Roman origin. Anne has previously described them like a 'power-house' of energy. We climbed to the top of the tallest mound and relaxed enjoying the warmth of the sun while discussing the matter. There were many pros and cons of different churches pointed out over the maps. We all tried dowsing to see if we could at least get the correct direction but this proved inconclusive. Still we got no further, but it had been an enjoyable excursion. Still aimless in our plans we set off again.

We thought we may have got the right place when, on the off chance we visited a small tumuli just north of Shudy Camps. Duncan and I had visited it before and had thought then that it had a pleasant, calming feel to it but this time it felt very oppressive and heavy. We all commented on the bad atmosphere and thought we may have found our sixth site. We conducted a meditation which involved raising the cone of power and then asking if this was the site visited by our opposing group. Finishing with a cleansing ritual we then brought down the cone again. Anne came out of the meditation quite dazed and stood staring in front of her at a depression in the ground. "I can see a group of people, they're all here in front of me but I don't think it's 'our lot'. They've got runes laid out on the ground in front of them, but no...... I don't think it's them." It seemed like everyone was at it but rather than detract ourselves from this quest by delving further into what this group were doing, we went on our way.

We were getting nowhere fast, what we've taken to calling Headless Chicken Syndrome was happening. Whilst talking we began to realise where we may have gone wrong. At most of the sites before, we had been given clues to the location of the next place while at the previous site. Perhaps what we had to do was return to Clare Castle and tune in again there. None of us were terribly keen on the idea, especially Anne who had been ill for a few days after our first visit there. However, on the plus side, this time it was full daylight and there would be other people around so perhaps it would be OK.

We set off for Clare and pulling into the packed car park we realised we certainly wouldn't be alone. Due to the adverse affects we had suffered last time, we found a quiet corner and conducted the Cabbalistic cross protection ritual (see Appendix) before going up to the summit of the hill.

Walking carefully along the path we soon reached the top and went to the spot behind the wall. It still felt very weird there but better than before. With children running by us we conducted a quick and quiet meditation. Anne came out and said that she'd seen the same church as before but this time she knew that there was also a well in the churchyard somewhere.

"Well the only church I know of with a well around here is Hadstock and that's quite a way away." said Richard, our oracle on churches in Essex.

As soon as Richard said Hadstock a sense of purpose came over

Our return visit to Clare Castle
where inspriation struck as to the location of the sixth site.
From left to right: Duncan, Richard, Anne, Cally, Brian and Jason D.

everyone. It seemed right. This had happened on a number of occasions during this quest. As soon as we had found the right site we all suddenly would seem quite positive about it, although none of us would quite know why.

Hadstock church is on the Michael line, a ley or energy line that runs from Carn Les Boels in Cornwall to Hopton on Sea in Norfolk and beyond off into the sea at either end. It also, like so many powerful places has a resident ghost; a pleasant old gentleman who has been seen by the Saxon doorway.

Off we set in a straight line west until just near the Cambridgeshire border. As we pulled up to the church Anne recognised it as the place in her vision. The curving driveway was just as she had seen it and there was a broken wall running around the perimeter of the churchyard which was the jagged shape she had seen.

First we wandered round inside the church and read the church guide. It informed us that St Botolphs was built in the late Anglo-Saxon period and was believed to be the resting place of St Botolph himself. We then looked at the maze design headstone for which Hadstock is noted. Lastly we all walked down to the holy well by the road, also dedicated to St Botolph. The proximity of the church to a holy well indicates that the site of church was probably considered sacred right back to pagan times. Our task now was to decide whether they had used the well for their magic or

Above: Hadstock church.

Below: Hadstock church's holywell.

somewhere in the churchyard. Anne wandered back and forth and seemed to settle for an area around the back of the church away from the road.

"There's something around here somewhere," she said indicating an area around a doorway and a yew tree, "it's like a seal for wax or something."

Search time again. Before long Duncan, who was busy looking in the foliage of the tree called out jubilantly. We all hurriedly gathered round as he pointed out a small ceramic object standing on a branch leaning against the trunk in the heart of the tree. Having stood aside for Richard and I to take some in-situ photographs, he retrieved the object. It looked like a pendant. It was clay and on one side was glazed green with two raised lines in the from of a V, which was obviously the seal Anne had seen in her mind. The other side was unglazed and had a faint cross on the back that looked like it had been lightly scribbled on with pencil. This artefact had the same magically charged feel to it which we all noted as we passed it around and was similar to that of the other artifacts. Once again Anne declined the offer to hold it until it had been cleansed.

Excited about our find we started to return to the well just to double check there had been no further desecration carried out there. On the way I asked Richard if I may look at the object again. This time I noticed a silver mark on the back of it as well as the cross that was there before. This appeared to have changed shape as well, it had grown two more lines

The area to the rear of Hadstock church where Anne felt there was a 'seal' concealed somewhere.

coming vertically from it, one from the top going out to the right, the other from the bottom going to the left. Everyone had a look and all agreed that the back had changed quite distinctly. The only explanation we could offer for this was that we had been standing in the shadow before and I was in the sunlight when I noticed the change. Returning into the shadow to look again, the silver mark was still quite clear so this was not the reason. It seemed something very odd had happened to the object. It was also worth noting that it was found in a Yew tree, a sacred tree traditionally associated with death and sadness.

Having checked the well, we carried out a cleansing visualisation before returning to the cars. We finished early as darkness was now falling and we had been out all day and a lot of petrol had been used. Despite our wish to complete a few sites in the day we weren't disappointed, as finding the artefact was highly rewarding. Anyone can easily question people's intuition or psychic information but the finding of physical confirmation can be less easily doubted. We now had three artifacts from this quest, as any quest goes these are impressive results.

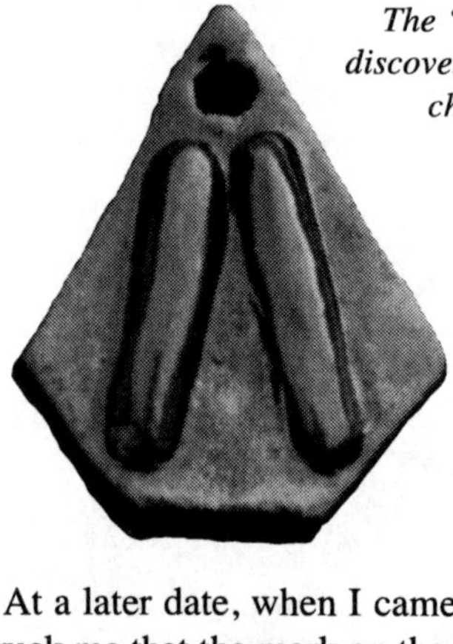

The 'seal' artefact discovered in Hadstock churchyard.

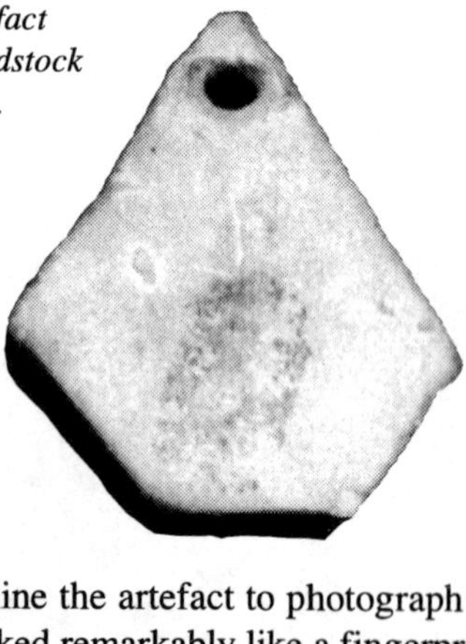

At a later date, when I came to examine the artefact to photograph it, it struck me that the mark on the back looked remarkably like a fingerprint of the glaze on the other side of the object or possibly a sticky patch left by the removal of a price tag. These both seem neat logical reasons for the mark, which after the event are very tempting to accept as the truth and ignore the opinions of the time. However, as we instantly took no photographs of this side of the object and have nothing but our own memory of events to rely on, it seems the mystical appearance of this mark has come into question. Even I myself who was totally and wholly convinced that it wasn't there when we first found the object now find myself bowing to the logical reason of 'it must have been' as it does so resemble a fingerprint, a very reasonable thing to have on the underside of a clay object which must, when being glazed, get a bit mucky.

Moving on to consider the markings on the pendant I tried to find a meaning to the runic kind of cross which was also on the underside of the pendant. The nearest symbol I have found to its appearance is that of the rune known as Wolfsangel. This is an additional rune from the Elder Futhark runic alphabet meaning ia (or ai in other books). The name and shape of this rune comes from an implement called a wolf hook from medieval times used to capture and torture wolves. The connotation of this rune is therefore similar and represents capture binding, blocking and restraint. It is closely related to another rune, that of the *yew* rune Eoh which has a similar woeful quality. The symbolism behind this rune is clearly not for the good, as there's not much call to be capturing wolves in modern day Hadstock.

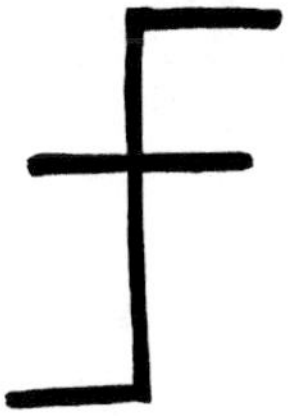

The form of the shape faintly drawn in pencil on the back of the 'seal'.

The rune Wolfsangel.

The mystery of what the raised V shape on the front side of the ceramic was eventually solved by Richard. He found that it relates to Y in the 'Dotted' runic alphabet from around 1300 - 1600. This rune of YR relates to a bow. Bows are symbolic of both hunting and divination and are made from wood of the *yew* tree. It also signifies protection at the expense of others. All this only went to confirm what we already felt we knew. That this coven was using magic in a very negative and corrupt way.

Chapter Six

THE BLACK DEMON OF THE TEMPLE

Following the pattern we had now found worked, we returned to Hadstock to try and gain some clues as to where to go next. On Wednesday 31 August we once again returned to the spot where we had retrieved the artefact. Duncan and I already had an idea in mind where we may go next from some map scouring and discussion amongst ourselves. We knew we would now be probably turning to a more southerly direction and only one place seemed to be a reasonable possibility, and that seemed a little too close but it was all we had to go on. However, we kept quiet so we wouldn't influence any psychic material which may be picked up. Much to Anne's annoyance, this would often be the case. We wouldn't let her in entirely on our discussions so if we were throwing ideas around we wouldn't be responsible for putting those impressions into her head.

It was just starting to spit with rain as we settled down to prepare for a meditation. With the artefact placed in the middle of our circle, we raised a cone of power and began the meditation to try and identify the next site. Anne said she could see us all going down a dark tunnel. There was a small shed near by and another building which she described as being like a standing stone.

Duncan and I passed looks of 'this seems hopeful' between us and quizzed Anne further.

"Might the building be a kind of domed temple and the tunnel be an avenue of trees on a hill? Instead of going down a tunnel as if going underground, you're maybe seeing us walking down hill," Duncan asked.

"Yeah, it could be. Why?"

We went on to describe to everyone a place called Ring Hill that we had visited before, overlooking Audley End House near Saffron Walden. It is an ancient hill-fort, believed to be of Iron Age origin, with an earthwork enclosing six an a half acres around the hill's summit. The entire hill is wooded except for an area in the centre where there is a house, with a shed very close to the path. There is also a large folly similar to a circular Grecian temple, built as a memorial to a war. This folly has a domed roof and steps and pillars running all the way around; the general shape of it could well be compared to that of a standing stone. We all agreed that it sounded like we had found the seventh site to be visited.

The path leading up to Ring Hill which Anne had psychically interpreted as a tunnel.

It was dark and raining heavily by the time we all pulled into a field entrance at the base of the hill opposite the long straight track up to the earthwork and house. Shining our torches up the track so Anne could see ahead of us, she confirmed that this was the 'tunnel' she had seen. As we walked along, we all found ourselves becoming anxious. The trees bowed down low and menacingly and the path seemed endless and we continued up and up, never seeming to get closer to the summit. Cally commented that she didn't want to walk at the back as she didn't like it. Thinking to myself that she was being silly, I dropped back, being brave, and walked alongside her. I instantly found myself agreeing with her, it felt as if there was definitely *something following us*. It was a feeling similar to that which you get when you know someone is looking at you, only very much stronger. We hurried on our way taking the path round to the right towards the folly. On nearing the building Duncan pointed out that we had given ourselves no protection. We all tried to ignore the creeping fear we were all experiencing and paused to conduct the Cabbalistic cross ritual, to prevent any ill effects happening to us on a psychic level. Never looking behind us we hurried on. Arriving at the folly we all turned to look at the path we had just taken. Anne and Richard could both see a demon-like creature, about 4 feet tall, ugly and very black. This was clearly the cause of our discomfort and was a very strong presence, as we could all sense it if not see it, even those of us not known for our psychic ability.

"What's it doing Anne?" I questioned.

"Just standing there looking at us," she replied, pointing to a spot a few metres away from where we all stood. "It doesn't move until we do. It's just standing there."

Once we had ascertained that it was making no move towards us, we continued on to stand on the temple steps. None of us daring to venture more than a few feet away from the rest of our group. We were all feeling both very aware and wary of this being but turned our attention to the site itself. Anne became quite giddy and said she could see all the group members here walking around the circular base of the folly inside of the pillars. We had to undo whatever is was they had done by walking round ourselves in the opposite direction. This we did while casting nervous glances all around us. However, it didn't seem to help the atmosphere or weaken the thought-form any, who had followed us as we walked round. Anne could now see thin lines of energy running from each of our Cabbalistic crosses towards it. Had we not raised them then it would have been feeding off our auras instead. This could leave you feeling very

Ring Hill Temple,
where we encountered a dark demon-like creature.

drained and sick. It seemed clear to us that this creature had been set up by a magical ritual they had carried out here and it had to be got rid of. The quicker the better, as we were all feeling quite ill and very uncomfortable at this place.

Huddled in a tight bunch we all stood facing the demon and prepared to conduct a visualisation to banish it. Richard started to speak, "In front of us see a spark of fiery light. Use this to draw out a pentagram in your minds........ Once you've completed that see it grow in size and strength getting brighter and more powerful........ Then move it towards the creature, see it force it backwards. Push it away faster and faster until it has forced the demon far from the site, far from the ground and finally off into outer space."

The atmosphere after this meditation was transformed, it became instantly much lighter and cleaner. Anne could still see traces of energy where the thought form had been but it had been thoroughly blasted out of existence. We all breathed a sigh of relief and began to relax and joke about the experience, even though it had been no laughing matter. Anne meanwhile had drifted off again. She could also see a lady dressed in white who called herself Brigit: she told Anne that she thanked us for our help. Brigit is usually a goddess often associated with wells but it seemed somehow she had been bound here as the guardian figure of Ring Hill Temple.

Pleased at our success at exorcism we continued on to find out about any possible artifacts and clues to our next stopping point. Anne felt that because they had done a full ritual here, they had left the 'black nasty' instead of any objects. When asked about the next site, we called on Brigit to help. She said, through Anne, that we were looking for a small square ruin and that we were to go over a stream and see a circle of trees on the side of a hill. There would also be a church to one side and some houses to the other. This looked like it would take a lot of map searching. We all felt fairly drained by our nights work so we agreed that we would save inspecting the map for next time.

Chapter Seven

HEADLESS CHICKEN SYNDROME

It was a week later on Wednesday, 7 September when we again met. Guessing at the location roughly on the map before hand, we arranged by phone to meet at Little Hadham; this was south-west of Ring Hill and roughly level with Coggeshall. Our next location would probably be there or somewhere near by. Duncan and I had been discussing the quest with a friend of ours, Andrew Tate, and although he is a complete non-believer in the mysteries, he nevertheless became hooked at helping us pre-guess the places before we found them. He had suggested a place near Hadham Ford where there is a large earthwork, so we tried there first. We had no idea what these large banks were for and although they were marked with hatchings on the map, no mention was made of them being ancient. We wandered along the track looking expectantly at Anne. "No this doesn't feel right; I can't see my circle of trees here."

Returning to the cars having tried our one possible site we started staring at the map again. There were no ruins marked in the area at all. Each of us were pointing to churches that were near rivers, or circular woods that were near churches. Nowhere seemed to have all the criteria that was in roughly the correct area of the map. We noticed an earthwork (which this time was marked as ancient) on the map in some woods not far away towards Westland Green. Setting off we didn't expect much success as earthworks in woods are hard enough to find in the daylight, let alone on a dark night such as this one. When we arrived we were greeted by an unfriendly local who informed us it was a private road and let it be known we weren't welcome. Thinking it had been a bad idea anyway we gave up on that one.

Back at Hadham Ford we conducted a meditation. No one could come up with any more clues to the location or even if we were in the right area. The two Jasons both suggested that perhaps the group hadn't visited the eighth site yet. We thought we had been catching them up, so was it possible that we had over taken them? Anne agreed that this may be the case and would explain why we couldn't find the venue of their latest desecration. However, with some more time left of the evening we didn't give up yet. We decided to move our map searching further afield. We would wear that patch out with all our looking. A church in Much Hadham started to look hopeful; there was a river, some trees and a few houses near-by but still no ruin. This made the distance from Ring Hill to there longer than any jump we had made so far. Still, we had already decided not to pay too much attention to geographic accuracy, only to use it as a guide for a starting point. It looked like it would be worth a try.

Having missed the turning twice we eventually found the church of St Andrew's to the east of the B1004 down a little lane. Anne recognised the shape of the spire instantly, perhaps we had found the eighth site after all. We were puzzled though, this churchyard didn't feel desecrated, it had the same peaceful atmosphere it should have. This certainly seemed to strengthen the thought that we had over taken them. There was only one way to find out and that was to return at a later date, in daylight when we could also check if there was the ruin and circle of trees near by. We would have to make sure that we left enough time before our next visit for them to have completed their ritual or laying of the artefact. None of us fancied the idea of bumping into these characters while about their work. Especially if they knew of us in the same way we knew of them, neither of us would probably be pleased at meeting the other, knowing of our opposing positions.

Chapter Eight

BACK ON TRACK

Having decided to leave the quest for a few weeks it was a month later on Thursday, 6th October when we could take up the pursuit again.

Anne and her husband Brian had gone out on a previous weekend to Much Hadham for a walk to see if this indeed was our next site or not. In the daylight Anne found the circle of trees, the near by stream and identified it as the correct church. All the elements of her vision were there except for the ruin. She was however sure that it was the right place. She did no psychic work at the site then, preferring to wait until we were all together.

On this occasion our numbers had dwindled as Big Jason was now unable to come and join us as often due to work and family commitments. We first re-visited Ring Hill, on this occasion to check out some information we had been given by some other members of Earthquest. At the previous meeting Geoff Webb and Wayne Frostick had asked us if we knew anything about Ring Hill. They had visited there and received the information that a woman dressed in white was being held there against her will in some kind of magical triangle. Thinking this woman was probably Brigit who had helped us on our last visit, we decided to check out what they said, in case Brigit needed our help. Possibly, we speculated, our opposing group had returned to recommit their desecration.

The atmosphere at Ring Hill was greatly improved since our last visit. Now in the cold light of day the whole scene looked so calm, with its glorious view out over Audley End House. It now seemed hard to imagine the unnerving experience we had all gone through.

We carried out a meditation to find out if what we had been told was true and what we could do about it if it was. Anne felt that Brigit wasn't trapped but was very unhappy. She was told by her, that people had left bad thought imprints over her temple and this had upset her. During this meditation Anne also picked up on some words, re-capping after the meditation she started quoting, "By the rivers of Babylon, where we sat down... What the devil does that mean?"

It was at this point that the rest of us, all laughing burst into song, singing the old Boney M hit from the seventies. With silly voices and dancing, we mucked about singing bursts of the song and wondering what it could mean. It seemed it didn't have to mean anything though. We had somehow pressed the temple's happy button by saying the magic words, and Brigit seemed content once again. With a job well done and the site thoroughly cleaned up we, still singing, descended the hill ready to set off to Much Hadham. Why a Boney M song had done the trick we've no idea but it worked and ours is not to question why.

With the winter nights now starting to draw in rapidly, it was twilight by the time we pulled up at St Andrew's. We scrunched our way along the gravel path as Anne explained that behind the church were some woods which formed a circle and that in the daylight she could identify it as definitely the place she had seen in her vision. We paused to let Anne tune in and contemplate any messages the site may have to give her and to assess the atmosphere. She couldn't work out where we should head for; the woods or the churchyard. She felt they were both important. Being already in the graveyard we started to wander around there first. In the half-light we all commented on a large tree, which in silhouette, resembled a giant. Bearing 'him' in mind for future use we

St Andrews at Much Hadahm.
The site we believed to be the eigth point on the web.

continued on towards the back wall. On the way we passed by a small low square wall that surrounded two low tombs.

"This is it," cried Anne "it's not a ruin its just a low wall, but it's definitely what I saw."

The overgrown tomb surrounded by a low wall in Much Hadahm churchyard, where Anne felt another artefact had been left.

Great! We all felt we were well and truly back on course. During a meditation we first called upon protection in the form of the Cabbalistic cross, then we asked for any clues about whether there was an artefact and if so where was it's exact location. Anne felt there was a small cross, silver in colour here and she could she a haze of light over the easterly half of the square enclosure. She also got the sense that they had conducted a ritual in the woods behind the churchyard before coming down to lay the artefact somewhere inside this low wall. This would explain why she couldn't decide which place was most important.

The search was on, and indeed it went on and on and on, but look as hard and as carefully as we might we couldn't find anything. Anne was sure something was still hidden there, as she had another one of her side effects of being near these kind of magically charged objects; a terrible stomach-ache. We tried another couple of meditations. One more simple tune in revealed nothing new. In the other we raised the cone of power and tried to contact any guardians of the site. For this we tried calling on the giant figure in the tree who we asked for help and to aid us in cleansing the site.

After this second meditation we all noticed the atmosphere change dramatically for the worse. I felt as if we weren't alone and a cold shiver of unease kept travelling along my spine. When I mentioned this to Anne, she said there was a mass of eyes watching us from the woodland. It appeared that we had inadvertently set something off or provided extra energy for their negative use. This churchyard had suddenly become very creepy, leaving me in no doubt that this was the place they had visited, artefact or no artefact.

On the subject of where to next, Anne had seen an isolated ruin or tower near a canal. This was proving tricky as Essex and it's surrounding area is rather short of this kind of thing, but we would have to take a look at the maps.

In the end we had to admit defeat and accept that if there was an artefact it had fallen in between the cracks in the tomb and was well underground, or possibly it had already been removed by the group only having been left for a short time. Disappointed, but eager to leave since the eyes started watching, we decided instead of carrying on any further we would retire to the nearest pub to consult the maps over some liquid refreshment.

Chapter Nine

THE NET

We had originally all arranged to meet at a Latton Priory ruin just south-east of Harlow, but all our plans changed when we got a phone call from Anne. She had a dream about the quest and now had a better idea of where we were going next. So on Wednesday 12 October we all met back up again at Much Hadham. On approaching the churchyard Duncan and I could see Anne and Richard busy poking around the edge of the tomb again. 'Never give up hope of finding something,' seemed to be a strong thought in Richard's head.

"Hello, have you found anything new?" Greetings were returned and heads were shaken in response to my question. "Where's Jason and Cally?" I added after a few more minutes of idle chat.

"Oh, they're not coming. He phoned me up earlier, he's got flu." replied Anne. So now we had just four to our number. Jason D was also now to only come out on some of our trips as he had recently also received a back injury at work. Understandably he wasn't that inclined to come and spend his evenings wandering around damp churchyards or similar.

"So what was your dream about then Anne?" Duncan prompted and Anne proceeded to fill us in on the contents of her dream. She had seen shire horses, a canal, a church not too far away, a beautiful garden and a tower. This place sounded as though it would be impossible to find with all those criteria, but Anne went on to explain how she knew roughly where it was. She had been talking with her sister about our outings and her sister had asked where we were going to next. Anne had replied that she didn't know but explained her dream and said it's somewhere with all those things.

"You must know where that is," Anne's sister had exclaimed, "we used to keep the canal boat there. You're seeing the horse that used to pull the barges. There was a tower near by there somewhere." The place she was referring to was Hoddesdon in Hertfordshire. This meant the line of the web on the map continued on in a south-westerly direction when we had expected it to turn in to the south-east. However, the clues fitted so we would try there. Questing works like that sometimes, fate takes a hand and points you in a certain direction. 'Go with the flow' is a good motto in questing. Anne couldn't remember where their houseboat used to be kept exactly but we had our area to begin the search in.

Having stopped on the way to buy a Luton and Hertford OS map we looked for the most likely place at which to start. There were two buildings marked that seemed probable; one was Netherhall at Roydon, a ruined gatehouse with a moat and the other was near a railway line at Rye House and just marked 'gatehouse'. The first seemed more appropriate so off we set.

Pulling up at the fifteenth century gatehouse at Netherhall we realised it wasn't the sort of place where they would go to conduct a ritual, as it was in the front garden of a beautiful farmhouse. Although we knew this couldn't be the right place, we stayed a while to admire the ruin, which was currently having restoration work carried out. Back at the map we pondered and considered our information. The fact that Anne knew she could see a canal from the tower wasn't much to go on as the area is absolutely covered with canals. The other gatehouse looked very built up around it so we weren't sure if that would be right. We drove round to a little church in the area of Broxbourne to try a meditation on more suitable ground. Unfortunately we gained nothing new from the exercise. I suggested that if the esoteric methods of communication weren't doing the trick, let's cheat and use a more terrestrial method. Unfortunately, phoning Anne's sister didn't help us as she couldn't remember the exact place where their houseboat was moored either. Having driven round to find a call box we were now on our way towards Rye House so we went to try there next.

Anne climbed out of the car nodding as she looked over at the gatehouse. "This is better: if we can find the canal then I'll be sure." We pointed out that one of the bridges which we had just driven over was above a canal. It seemed this was the place; we had found the ninth site.

Although there were buildings around, none of them were close and the gatehouse, which dates from the fifteenth century, stood in a large area of grass which doubled as a picnic area, surrounded by a square moat. We all wandered around looking at the original ground plan of the building when it was complete, now marked out in brick paths. There was a large outer wall which would have surrounded the garden. Perhaps Anne had

Rye House, which Anne had psychically identified as the next site by the canal running behind the grounds.

been seeing how the garden may have looked back in past times. The notice board informed us that the Gatehouse was at the centre of attempted treason when in 1683 it housed a group of Cromwell's supporters conspiring to kill Charles II and his brother.

We came to a spot around the far side of the building and Anne commented that the energies of the site were all in a spin because she could see a number of the group here performing a rite which involved them all moving in an anti-clockwise direction while holding hands. This circular movement was

Below: The area to the rear of the Gatehouse where the energies felt highly unbalanced.

probably to activate the energies of the site. Creating a whirlwind effect awakens the energy flow and enlivens it into a form which can then be worked with. We also use this effect when creating our own cone of power but we always ensure that once we have finished we take down the cone and dissipate away any excess energy otherwise this kind of after-effect can be left behind. The natural energy of a site is thrown into disruption and a sensitive like Anne can sense this disruption. Almost certainly non-psychics can also be affected by this kind of energy disturbance but do not realise the cause of their possible irritation, discomfort or bad mood. Anne insisted that to calm the energies, we must all do likewise, except we must move in the opposite direction to try and counteract the effects of this motion.

After a protection ritual we linked hands and solemnly walked around against this flow of unbalanced energy and try in our minds to calm it. Once this exercise was completed we commenced a meditation close to the wall. Both Anne and Duncan felt very giddy during this session, probably due to this whipping up of the energies which our opposing group had caused.

"There's a net. I can see a net has been thrown over this whole site," Anne said in a quiet worried tone, once we had all been silent for a few minutes.

"Do you see any site guardians at all Anne?" Richard enquired.

"Yeah, she's trapped too.... She's a young nun, we've got to help her."

"OK, we'll try and break the net." Richard said as he began to guide us through the cleansing exercise. "Use the same column of light which we brought down for our protection and see it begin to move out across the site..... Picture glowing strong white light..... See this burning the net away and cleansing the gatehouse and its grounds..... Take it right out to the moat and beyond....... See it cleanse the trees, the building, the air....... See it penetrate into the ground..... Everything is glowing and the net is burned away. Now bring the light back into the column leaving everything touched with a faint etheric glow........"

Having completed this exercise we went on to the subject of the next site.

"I can see a bridge with grass both over and underneath it." Anne's voice was becoming quite weak as the dizziness she was suffering obviously grew worse. "I know where it is." She then sat down on the ground to try and steady herself. We hurriedly brought and end to this meditation. While we were coming out of the session Duncan felt something fall on him; he described it like a blanket being thrown over his head. Thinking this was part of the net we re-visualised the net-breaking light once again, especially over Duncan. Afterwards we discussed this strange occurrence and the information received. Anne felt there was no artefact left at this place, only this etheric net. The net may possibly have been set up as a trap to ensnare us and prevent us following their path and disrupting and interfering with their work. This net could also be seen as another form of the web as they both have a lot of symbolism in common. They are both symbols of ensnaring and entanglement and also both represent negative aspects of the Great Mother. They probably hoped we would not know of it, but with Anne's psychic material and Duncan's physical sensation we were fully aware of their ensnaring and were consequently able to combat it.

During the meditation Anne also got a name for the group. She felt they were calling themselves the circle or ring of Adandara. What or who Adandara* is we don't know despite a lot of searching (any suggestions gratefully received). Once again though we were back to the circle imagery, representing the wheel of existence, life and death cycles etc.

The bridge Anne had seen was in the gardens of Copped Hall. Richard too knew of this place and was obviously relishing the idea of returning there. It is a large burnt out mansion, visible from the M25 near Epping, with a deserved reputation for occult activity and dodgy goings on. We had all joked previously that we may have to call there. Anne and Richard had visited it on previous occasions and last time they had black demons growing out of the cellar floor in front of them! Richard thought this was great fun but Anne was less keen.

Anne recovered quickly and we took a break to go for some chips and decide whether to brave this awesome place in the dark or wait until daylight. It was still fairly early and the idea of having the run of a haunted ruin to ourselves sounded quite fun. We settled on the idea that we would go and have a look but do no psychic work, as any further drain on Anne would not be a good idea. So we set off south-west, bound for Epping.

After the half a mile walk to the hall Duncan and I were in no way disappointed by the way the others had described it. The grounds have two temple like summer houses set at split levels and the house is huge and imposing. There are beautiful carvings to be found all around, tucked away on pieces of remaining architecture and on the main building. We didn't enter inside as in it's ruined condition it looked a bit unsafe to blunder

* As psychic information can never be relied on to be absolutely correct it is worth looking at similar words. Richard found one such word in a Kenneth Grant book. It was the name on a Priestess of Maat working in Ohio in the 1970's, Andahadna. However none of the text relating to this woman ties in at all with the events of the web. There is some talk of spiders but also of many other animals so I don't really think it can be considered a likely connection.

In asking around I have also heard of a dark serpent creature called Adandra, possibly from Hindu magic, but have been unable to confirm this.

around in the dark. Besides, the graffiti over the door saying 'Welcome To Hells Gate' seemed a bit **too** appropriate. Anne mentioned that she could see a knight who patrols up and down between the two follies, he apparently appears quite happy with his perpetual task. It was the most amazing place to wander around at night and we all lost ourselves in searching around this forgotten little world.

Chapter Ten

GARDEN OF MYSTERY

Copped Hall is a place steeped in history. Epping Forest is very close and once must have covered the land which the hall is built on. Neolithic man was living in the forest 4,000 years ago and left his mark on the landscape. Almost along the line of the present day Lodge Road, which connects Epping Road to the gates of Copped Hall, he built a causeway using logs. In doing this a stream was blocked and thus created a bog which is still there today. Also, in a field to the side of the hall are the remains of an Iron Age hill fort.

The hall itself, the third on the site, was built by Thomas Heneage, Treasurer to Queen Elizabeth I and was visited by many monarchs in its day. Now it stands as a burnt out shell due to a fire on Sunday, 5th May 1917, thought to have been caused by a hair clip used as a fuse wire.

When we returned to Copped Hall on Sunday, 16th October we realised it wasn't the forgotten world we had originally liked to think. Many people were cycling or wandering around alone or with families. This somehow didn't suit the hall and its grounds and certainly wasn't very conducive to the work we had to do for the quest, despite the fact we had been to other busy places and not been bothered by company.

Having all clambered through a window at the side of the building we started exploring. Now in the light of day, we headed straight for the cellars. It seemed probable it would have been there that the group had performed any rites, or left any artifacts as they are the most secluded part of the whole complex. Torches out we started down the network of corridors. The scene that greeted us was like that from an American gang film. The walls were a mass of graffiti, while beer cans and the like were strewn everywhere. While shining our lights around we were all surprised

Above: Copped Hall the back aspect which can be seen from the M25.

Left: The ruined facade of the front of the hall.

that the atmosphere didn't feel too bad, no worse than any dark, damp place. We continued on and as we once again came out into the daylight Anne was sure they had not visited the cellars.

We wandered slowly round the rest of the ruin before returning to the gardens to check out the bridge that Anne had seen during the meditation at Rye House. This felt more probable she thought, but still she wasn't exactly sure. We also searched around the nearest summer house. This pair of follies were built by Charles Eamer Kempe in the middle to late

The bridge in the grounds of Copped Hall
which Anne had psychically seen while in meditation at Rye House.

The two storey folly, in the lower room of which we were visited by a presence.

Detail of the statue on the folly.

The bridge and the folly beyond. Between which Anne felt the 'Queen' had held her ritual. Also the raised walkway to the left where the queen had been prevented from going any further by the guardian knight.

nineteenth century. The one we were searching featured two large statues of men holding goats or rams heads on either side of the entrance. The lower level of this folly also felt likely thought Anne; she was torn between the two not being able to clearly see exactly where they had been. To try and sort this out we did a meditation in the lower room of the folly. We raised the cone of power and sent light out to clean the site. As we were doing this Anne, Richard and myself all felt a cold shiver up our spines as another presence came through the room. Anne afterwards said, "It wasn't happy about us cleaning the place up but I don't think it was anything to do with the 'circle'." She went on, "I think they've used both places. I can see the group walking between them. They couldn't get to the house because of the knight, he was stopping them." He was obviously good at his job of guardian spirit.*

We had searched everywhere we could and Anne had tried to tune in

* When we returned to Copped Hall at a later date to take photographs, Anne could once again see the knight, as she had on all other previous visits. It was an afternoon one weekend and once again there were some visitors wandering the ruins. A couple of women were standing some way away from us along the knights walkway and Anne was relating his position to us in a vain attempt for us all to try and see him. Quite unprompted the two women stepped back out of his path as Anne described his approach. There was no other reason for their behaviour other than the fact that some part of all of us must be able to sense things beyond our vision and understanding.

to where exactly an artefact (if any were there) would be hidden but there was just too many distractions for her to be able to concentrate properly. She did manage however to get some information on where we were to go next. In her mind's eye she could see an isolated church which was very dark both in aspect and actual colour; this was next to some woods and there was a dried up ditch near by. Anne could also see a head which looked different from the normal sort of carving or painting you would find in a church. We guessed that this church would be somewhere in the Brentwood area as the web was now turning in a more easterly direction to go across the base. Looking at the map so many churches looked like possibilities, while none stood out as being particularly likely. We would just have to go around visiting them all until Anne would hopefully recognise the right one.

St Marys and All Saints of Lambourne was our first stop as it was in the right direction and on the way towards the others should it prove to be wrong. This apparently looked very similar in shape to the church which Anne had seen. Not daring to think we might have found the eleventh site straight away, we conducted a brief meditation. No one however got the feeling there had been any desecration done to this site at all and there was no woodland as Anne had seen. Perhaps it wasn't right after all.

Bearing Lambourne church in mind we next visited Brentwood Country Park. We had difficulty finding this little church hidden in the trees as darkness had now fallen. As it turned out, it was actually in someone's front garden. This was a beautiful little church with a serene atmosphere and consequently clearly not the destination we were looking for in our quest. On returning to the cars we found we had company. Two policemen were waiting for us and obviously thought we were all on drugs! We just explained that we were lost and hadn't seen the signs which stated that the park was closed after dark. Then thinking we were mad instead, they sent us on our way. Taking this as our cue to call it a night and go in search of this elusive church another day, we said our goodbyes.

CHAPTER ELEVEN

PSYCHIC STABBING

On the evening of Wednesday 26 October Anne, Richard, Jason D, Cally, Duncan and myself all congregated outside the church of St Marys at Stapleford Abbots; our next site to try with the pot luck method. Once again we all instantly agreed that this wasn't where the circle had been, the atmosphere held no hint of desecration. While here however, we used the sanctity of the churchyard to conduct a meditation to see if we could get more clues. Both Cally and myself could clearly see a church during this. Cally described her vision as having a very tall steeple and I saw a very low church, red in colour also with a steeple.

We were fast running out of suitable looking churches. I had a feeling about Navestock, but we had discounted it earlier thinking it was a little out of our search area. I suggested it again and we all decided to give it a go. On drawing up in the car park of St Thomas the Apostle that same 'this is it' feeling came over all of us. The church had a high thin steeple and a very low tiled roof, which was the red I had seen. The walls were rendered but when we found a patch where the render had come away, underneath there was the dark stone which Anne had described. There was a small copse of trees to the back of the churchyard and to one side Anne found the dried up ditch that she had mentioned. Inside the church she instantly recognised a monument in a chapel to the side. It featured a bust of the deceased and did look quite an unusual memorial for a church so, we also had found the unusual head. Everything fitted.

Having had a feel round the whole churchyard Anne settled for a sheltered corner at the back of the church. They had come here in a group and she could see them standing in a circle where we were now standing ourselves. We settled down to do a meditation to find some answers for this

Navestock Church of St Thomas the Apostle.

site and once again we used the Cabbalistic cross before going into a medative state.

Coming out of this meditation Anne turned to Duncan, "Well?" she simply said.

Duncan looked stumped, not quite sure what he was expected to say he ventured, "Well I've got all shivers up my back."

"I'm not surprised!" Anne exclaimed. "You've just been stabbed in the back. I saw one of 'them' come behind you and then stab you with a big knife."

We all stood agape at this turn of events. Why had they singled Duncan out, was what we all wondered? Was it because they had caught him in their net back at Rye House? Luckily he seemed to have suffered no ill effects from the experience.

Anne felt they had left an artefact here, a small sword and once again she had her stomach-pains. We all set to exploring the area. Investigating every hiding place we could find and searching the ground to find any signs of the earth having been disturbed to bury something. Despite our concerted efforts, we could unfortunately find nothing. As the next best thing to removing the artefact we did a cleansing meditation.

We went into the porch to discuss the events of the evening and find a comfortable place to sit to conduct a third meditation on the possible

The area to the rear of the churchyard where Anne psychically saw Duncan attacked and she felt another artefact may have been left..

whereabouts of the next location. This was also to not be a great success, as Anne could simply see a high brick wall which just had dense blackness beyond it.

"Oh great, a void," said Richard, very keen and all of a sudden perking up. "You go in Anne, we'll hold your legs," he said with his tongue firmly in his cheek. These 'voids' however are to be avoided (no pun intended) at all costs (unless your feeling foolhardy like Richard). They are basically like black holes of psychic nothingness which are potentially dangerous.

Anne's face dropped at his comment. She is far too gullible and falls for every wise crack Richard may make. We continued the wind-up by discussing linking her to us with an etheric rope so maybe she could see into it. Anne didn't look impressed, so we told her that perhaps on second thoughts it didn't seem like such a clever idea.

Having had a laugh we turned our attention back to the subject, Anne looked perplexed. She had obviously drifted off to wherever it is she goes when she attunes. "There's just nothing," she said coming out of her reverie, "no buildings or anything, it's just dark."

It was back to the maps for guess work time again. The web's thread would now probably be heading directly east and run for approximately half the distance between Navestock and the first site, East Hanningfield. It shouldn't be that hard to find.

The only place we could see that looked like a possibility was a tumulus in a nature reserve near Billericay called Norsey Woods, itself an ancient woodland. It was our only shot, so we went for it.

It was raining heavily when we pulled in along a side road by the dark woodland. Our footsteps squelching in the mud as we went we soon found the tumulus as both Richard and Jason D had been there before. Anne looked ponderous as she wandered around. "What's over that way," she asked as she pointed over further into the woods.

"Not a lot, just more trees," Richard replied.

Anne obviously felt that we were near. Over the opposite side of the wood was an official car park. So to get to the other side of the thick bank of trees surrounding the tumulus we went to move the cars round to there, thinking we could then approach it from the other side.

On returning to the cars we found we had the company of a man busily taking down all our registration numbers. As it turned out he suspected we were maybe out badger-baiting in the woodland. Annoying as somebody minding your business can be, we were pleased to see that someone was aware of the problem and ready to fight it.

Having fended off the mans questions and convinced him that we weren't blood thirsty morons we drove round to the main car park. Minding the puddles as we went we cut off the main path at the first opportunity. The path was quite distinct even in the dark and it led to a large clearing in amongst the sweet chestnut trees. This was we guessed fairly much just the other side of the tumulus. Anne was positive this was the place and indeed in the night, this clearing was very dark as all the trees blocked out even the star or moonlight. We had found the twelfth site which completed the web.

Everyone felt drawn to a particularly huge tree standing a little more proud than the others. However, it was getting late and we were all wet from the rain. It was decided it was best to continue on in the daylight and hopefully dry weather. We retired to The Griffin in Danbury (made famous by Andrew Collins' meetings with Bernard during the Black Alchemist saga) for some very welcome warmth, shelter and refreshments.

CHAPTER TWELVE

FULL CIRCLE

We returned on Sunday, 30th October complete with carrier bags in which to collect sweet chestnuts. Once again is was hammering down with rain but in true questing style we put up with it. The same tree instantly drew Anne again and she immediately started searching around in the leaves at the base while all the men searched around in the branches that splayed out right from the base. Cally and I were a way off busy collecting chestnuts but we paused to go and join the others. Anne had found a piece of bamboo cane poked into the ground and was using it to dig with. She called us all over as she saw something in the dirt and Richard removed it from the ground for her. *It was a slate with runic markings etched onto it.* All along Anne had been joking that she wanted to find something with runes on and here it was, her long awaited for artefact. We all held the slate and tried to make

The large chestnut tree which dominated the clearing, beneath which Anne uncovered two etched slates.

out what was on it but we would need to wash the dirt off before we could see clearly. Jubilant at this find we each took turns to try and make out the markings amongst the mud. Meanwhile, Anne had carried on poking around in the hole she'd made with a stick and after another minute she had uncovered a second slate. The **fifth** artefact we had found on this quest, these were **really** good results. These objects she wasn't as wary of touching, "They're very weak, this one has been here a long time." she said indicating one of the pair.*

As Anne held the slates she concentrated on them; she felt that this was the first location the group had used. This made perfect sense as we discussed the matter. When they came here they planted the first slate and marked its position with the piece of cane. They then carried out all their rituals and laying of artifacts all around Essex and its surrounding counties to set out their web. Finally they return to Norsey Woods to plant a second artefact to seal off the whole of the circle outside. Hence this is why there were two artifacts planted in the same place.

As we pondered this we thought it may be a good idea if we also returned to where we had started to close off our own web of positive energy. The other point we noted was that the piece of bamboo was only the second piece of visible evidence which we had found of the circles visits; the first being the chalk cross in Hatfield Peverel churchyard. If ever you do see evidence of ritual activity it is highly likely that the culprits are amateurs. If the practitioners of magic know what they're doing you will virtually never see a sign of their presence. It was only by the fact that we were specifically searching for evidence we found those two signs.

While walking back to the cars Richard washed the slates in a puddle but once soaked the colour of the stone was still too dark to depict anything very clearly. A few minutes above the car heater and we would be able to see the markings unobscured. The drive back towards our starting point seemed a long one. The rain pounded down as we navigated the dark winding lanes each lost in our own thoughts of the web and the completion of its outer ring.

* Some months later I thought to ask Anne why she felt she was able to hold these slates but none of the other artifacts we had found. She herself didn't know, she just knew that she couldn't feel the charge which she can sense coming off them. We discussed that perhaps the rain had cleansed them or maybe it was the fact they were totally buried, whereas both knives and the ceramic which we had found previously had been hidden amongst grass or in trees.

While we were talking something struck Anne. "I never touched the tree," she said as this revelation dawned on her. "I didn't want to, but I love trees and always feel them. Maybe the tree had taken up into it whatever was held in the slate. Do you remember I got Richard, Duncan and Big Jason to feel around in the branches." Now she mentioned it I did, and indeed it is unusual for Anne not to want to touch a tree. It seemed the energy that had been in the slates had been absorbed up through the roots into the tree.

The retrieval of state one (above) and slate two (below).

On returning to East Hanningfield we first gathered round Richard's car to see the results of what was on the now dry slates. On the first there was a row of 6 runic symbols and on the other side there was clearly marked a sun-like symbol; a large upturned U shape and another rune. On the second there was once again a row of runes, this time 7, and 1 other on the opposite side. It certainly looked like there was plenty of sifting through various rune books to be done to sort that lot out. Once our immediate curiosity had been satisfied, (we could concentrate on checking the meanings out later) we headed over to the small copse which held the old graveyard under its cover. Here we would conduct a full length meditation where we would travel around in our minds reaffirming the positive thoughts and cleansing which we had left behind us at every site. Having selected a clearing near the centre of the copse we all stood clear of the dripping bushes and prepared ourselves for the final stages of the outer ring of the web quest. Richard began to speak and our journey around the web began again, this time on a mental level.

Across the landscape we flew, seeing the Essex countryside unfold beneath us. One by one we revisited the sites locating them by landmarks and stopping briefly to spread a glow of light over each contaminated spot. Hopefully this would be wiping out any last trace of the desecration that had been done and would break down our opposing groups magical web completely. After we had visited Norsey Woods for the second time that day we made our way in our minds back to the spot in East Hanningfield where we had left our bodies standing in the rain.

"Did anyone get anything," asked Richard when we had all opened our eyes after the meditation. It had been a long session and we all initially commented that we felt dizzy and a bit 'out of it'. This feeling of disorientation is prone to happen after long meditations and it sometimes takes a while for your mind come totally 'back to earth' again.

Anne suddenly spoke softly, "Cast the runes, play the cards, syphilis be here, syphilis beware." She was staring off into space and was clearly not quite back with us yet. We all looked at one another highly perplexed that Anne should be picking up on sexually transmitted diseases during meditations. This had stumped us all; we hadn't the faintest idea what it could mean but it was the source of many jokes for the rest of the day. Shaking her head to wake herself up Anne mentally rejoined us and asked us to repeat what she'd said. As often happens when Anne comes out of deep meditation she is quite unaware of what has transpired. We filled her in but like the rest of us she too was totally oblivious as to this strange phrases meaning or origin.

The general consensus on the meditation was that it had worked well and the whole quest so far was a job well done. However, it wasn't finished yet. All along right from Anne's original sketch of the web there has been a thirteenth site, a central hub. We thought they may well have not actually visited the centre as Halloween (a highly likely night for them to conclude their work due to its magical potency) was on the following night, but Anne had succeeded in finding the site at Much Hadham before they had gone there so perhaps it could be found beforehand this time as well.

In a quick meditation Anne saw an isolated church or ruin and a sword, ritually placed blade down, into the ground. This once again wasn't much to go on but if they had used the centre on the map it would narrow down the area to scrutinize considerably.

Looking at our map with all twelve sites marked on it there was no mistaking that the Great Dunmow area was the geographical centre. We would concentrate our search there. We knew the church in Great Dunmow had houses very near by, so maybe Little Dunmow church would be a better place to begin our search for the centre.

When we pulled up at this pretty little country church dedicated to St Mary we realised that it would be an inappropriate site for the circle's purposes. Although standing by a large village green, the whole road opposite was full of brightly lit houses. We had a walk around while we discussed where we would head to next. Anne once again stressed she thought there might be a ruin near by.

"There's a ruin up at Tilty, perhaps we should try there," suggested Richard.

"We noticed that place when we were looking on the map the other day," I added, remembering that our friend Andy had suggested it a while ago as a possibility for the central site.

"Ah, there's a really weird church up that way as well. It's got a very strange aura and it's in the middle of nowhere. It's always open as well which is really good," said Richard having a sudden brain-storm of possibilities.

"OK. Sounds good, let's try there then," and with Anne's words we all headed back to the cars.

We tried Chickney church first. This is a redundant church so it is still kept open but no longer holds services. Dedicated to St Mary the Virgin it stands on the site of a circular burial ground that is believed to have had continuous burial since Saxon times. As Richard had said it certainly had a very strange feel to it. We went inside and strolled around shining our torches on points of interest. Anne said she felt very uncomfortable here and I was inclined to agree with her; it was quite eerie; this place definitely felt haunted. She felt this may possibly be where they planned to come but it definitely hadn't been desecrated by them yet. Commenting that this was just a naturally dark place we headed off to visit Tilty church.

This pretty country church is also dedicated to St Mary the Virgin and is about half a mile away from the remains of Tilty Abbey, a Cistercian Monastery dating from the twelfth century. There is now only one section of Abbey wall still standing.

Having parked on the grass at the back of the church we walked up the path and were surprised to find this church was also unlocked. The first thing we noticed on entering was the dreadful paint work. The pews were all painted bright blue; different, we thought. Anne once again wasn't sure; it could be where they were going to use but if it was they hadn't yet been.

While standing in the warm we took the opportunity to discuss our quest. The question we all wanted answered was what exactly was the purpose behind this group's desecrations. We will never get a complete answer to this question unless we ever met them personally (which I most certainly hope we don't). However, Anne could give us a small insight into this from her thoughts on the matter. "They're after power in the business world or politics; something like that. I think they're aiming to gain influence for themselves and others, in high places. This is all inside the web they've made." It seemed they were simply using their magic in a selfish manner by taking from sites and utilising the energy for their own use. In using the form of the web of fate they were trying to weave their own destiny and affect that of others.

It could be argued that we, in effect, do much the same thing when questing. We use the sites inherent energies to enable psychics to gain more information. There is one major difference though, and that is we always try and give a little back, a small boost of energy from ourselves. We also always thank any guardians and make sure we leave a place clean both on the physical and spiritual level.

Having debated the matter for a while we decided to call an end to the evening. Just as we were leaving we were suddenly covered in a blinding flash of light. Having sat in the church with only a few torch beams, Big Jason had suddenly found the light switch, revealing the paint work in all its full glory. Making final jokes about this unique style we went our separate ways home, all hoping for more success at finding the centre next time.

CHAPTER THIRTEEN

THE RUNES

A while later when I found the time, I did much fervent checking into books on runes to try and interpret what was written on the slates. Having never examined runes before, I also asked for the help of Wayne Frostick, another member of Earthquest, much wiser on the subject than I, to give me his opinion on them as well.

Runes are the major magical alphabet and originally come from Central and Northern Europe. They have many uses in the world of the occult from spell-binding to divination. Most of the characters weren't hard to find. They are part of the Elder Futhark runic alphabet, the oldest known complete runic alphabet and the most commonly used. The alphabet dates from the early fifth century and has 33 basic characters and some additional symbols for letter combinations.

Slate 1, side 1 we had already looked at. It was the side which features a large sun-like image with an upturned U and a rune below it. At a meeting we had discussed this pictogram amongst the whole group and it was agreed that the top symbol was definitely the sun and the two lines coming from one ray possibly represented the beginning and the end of the web, where the slates were found. The only problem we found with this reasoning was why were there only 8 rays or spokes coming from the centre rather than the expected 12 if it were to represent the web. However, these 8 lines could possibly represent festivals of the year such as the 2 equinoxes, the 2 Solstices and the 4 other major pagan festival; Beltane, Lammas, Samhain and Imbolc.

Below this solar symbol was a large upturned U shape and below that the rune Eihaz; representative of protection. Sun symbols? Protection? It all seemed a bit rosy to me to be from an artefact found on a black quest. I

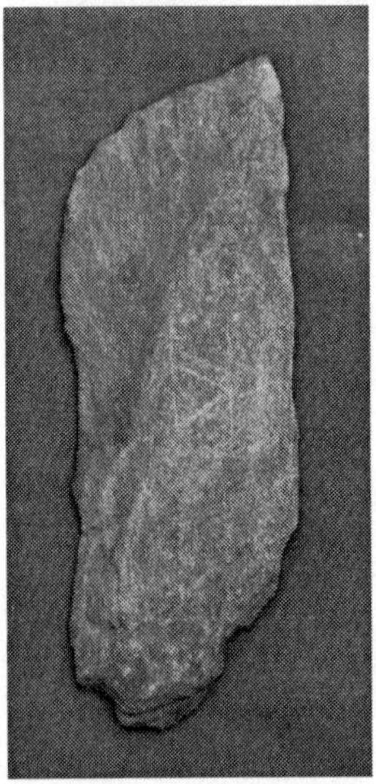

Above left: Slate one, side one.
Above right: Slate one, side two.
Left: Slate two, side one.
Below: Slate two, side two.

obviously hadn't got the right frame of mind for these things. As soon as Wayne explained his interpretation of its meaning to me it made sense. He reasoned that the large U shape represented the earth and the whole meaning of this image was to protect the earth from the power of the sun. In other words to cause a perpetual winter; a time ruled by darkness.

Side 1.

Side 2.

The runic markings etched onto the two sides of slate 1.

The other side of this first slate's inscription consisted of 6 runes, Eihaz, Odal, Wyn, Ur, Ken and Gyfu, which in letters spells YOTHUKG. Not much sense was to be made of that, so they obviously weren't using the literal phonetic meaning of the runes. When I read through the separate meanings of each rune I endeavoured to try and make some sense of it. Each rune had a number of meanings (in divination each direction the rune falls in alters the ideas and symbolism behind it) and many related aspects eg. trees and plants, gods, elements, seasons, etc. So which of each of these parts were relevant and made a whole? There were so many possible connotations it seemed to me it was like looking for a needle in a haystack. Once again Wayne proved me wrong by offering up what to me sounded like a very plausible interpretation. He suggested that in using the protection rune (Eihaz) first they are warding off unwanted influences (eg. the sun and spring) from the earth (represented by Odal, the ancestral land). They are then taking Joy (Wyn) at sacrificing the primal power (Ur) to the fire (Ken) as a gift to the gods (Gyfu). I had come across all these meanings

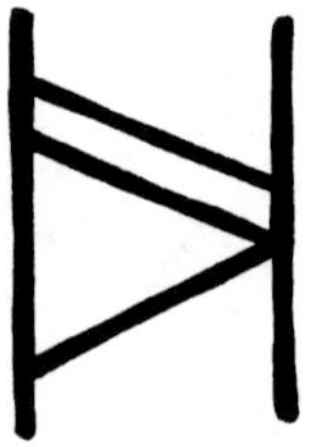

The runic marking on Slate2, side 1.

The runes Haegl (left) and Thorn (right). The two composite features of the mark on the slate?

on my travels through various books and his whole interpretation seemed sound to me.

Slate 2, side 1 was not as instantly easy to find until I read that any number of runes could be moulded together to create a new symbol with the joint meaning of it's composite features. Turning to the chart in one of Nigel Pennick's books I scanned it for possibilities. Two runes fitted perfectly to make a copy of that on the slate. Haegl and Thorn. Haegl is generally seen as the most disruptive of runes, by influencing the subtle web of wyrd it brings doom in the form of natural disasters. Meanwhile Thorn isn't much jollier in aspect. It represents the Hammer of Thor and is symbolic of a giant fierce demon and the evil force of disruption and chaos. They also both signify ice and winter. Both these runes are equally chaotic and disorderly and together must make a powerful runic symbol.

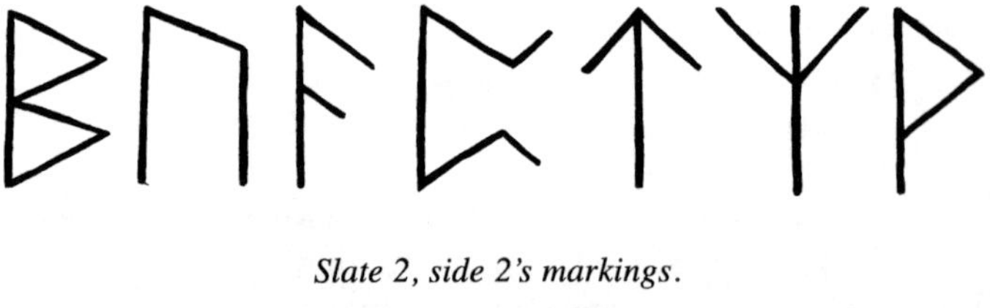

Slate 2, side 2's markings.

On the opposite side of this slate were once again all characters from the Elder Futhark alphabet. Beroc, Ur, As, Peorth, Tyr, Eihaz and Wyn.

(This by the way spells BUAPTZW!) Wayne's interpretation of these seemed to me to be a little less clear than the first but fitted nevertheless. He said, the fertility rites of spring (Beroc) are a sacrifice of primal power (Ur) to the gods (As), or perhaps a sacrifice to the primal power of the gods. A game is being played (represented by Peorth) with the Sky God (Tyr) and the web makers have protection (Eihaz) and finally joy and glory (Wyn).

The first of these slates therefore seems to very much represent a warding off and suppression of spring while the second slate shows directly disruptive runes, once again related to repressing spring. Also returning to Slate 1, side 1's solar symbol I now reconsidered the 2 lines coming from the lowest ray. This could possibly represent a block at the spring equinox (21 March) or perhaps Beltane (May day).

As I have stressed runes represent quite vague symbolism; raw and waiting to have certain implications put on them by their surrounding characters and the person who casts them. Therefore in their very nature, they are a highly individual thing, having different interpretations to different people.

These slates would have their greatest effect put in a place surrounded by nature, dependant on the sun and coming of spring. So where better for the 'Queen of Spades' and her company to position them than in a clearing in a wood. A spot which come spring should be teaming with life and energy.

The implications of the discovery of these slates were great. Our opposing group was warped and ambitious if their ideal world consisted of an endless season of winter.

CHAPTER FOURTEEN

THE SEARCH FOR THE CENTRE

On the evening of Wednesday, 2nd November we all congregated once again at Chickney church having decided that of the two churches we visited it was the most feasible and was somewhere we could all find again. Duncan and I were first to arrive and as we waited in the car Duncan suddenly started. "God, I just thought I saw a cat right outside the window. It's eyes were glowing," he said, quite shaken and clearly convinced of what he'd seen. It actually turned out to be a branch of the tree we were parked under, overhanging the car. We went on talking when suddenly. "What was that!" he exclaimed. "I thought I heard footsteps." I myself had thought I heard something strange at this point too, but it wasn't footsteps. Now he'd got me feeling jumpy too. This was definitely a very spooky place. Not long afterwards we saw lights coming up the track as the others arrived in Big Jason's Sierra.

"Alright, how's it going?" we were greeted by Jason. We explained the couple of frights Duncan had received that evening.

"Yeah? I had a strange thing happen to me this morning. I was just pulling out of where I work, when a hawk came and flew right up to the van window. It just missed the glass. It scared the hell out of me." said Jason.

It seemed it was the day for weird occurrences. Perhaps we were being paranoid thinking these things could be anything to do with the 'opposition party' but you never know.

We once again returned to the church to see if the atmosphere felt any different to when we were there on the previous Sunday. It was now passed

Halloween and if, as we suspected, they had now completed their web, then Anne would be able to tell if this was where they had been.

She stood looking pensive for a while as we all wandered around the church lighting a few of the candles. "No, this isn't it, I don't like it here but it's not the place."

We could all see that dreaded syndrome coming on again, 'Decapitated Poultry Syndrome' as we'd sometimes call it for a change. We had tried a few of the choices we felt likely but had unfortunately got nowhere. It was decided that we would do a meditation to see if we could gain any more information on what it was exactly we were looking for. We all took seats in the pews and sat in a silence in the candle-lit church. As we all came out of our mediative state there was a lot of shaking of heads. No-one seemed to have received any useful information. This was probably not helped by the fact that Stansted Airport is not far away and a plane was coming in to land low over the church during the meditation. Duncan and Anne had both heard a low chanting but this was probably simply some 'site memory' and unfortunately was no use to us in the quest.

Anne sat quietly for a few more moments while the rest of us were playing silly-buggers with torch lights on the ceiling. "What's at Great Leighs?" she enquired, "I've only ever been to the show ground." The show ground Anne was referring to was the Essex showground which is situated off the main road through Great Leighs.

"A couple of churches, St Anne's Castle, the old pub with the witches stone outside, a tunnel running from there to somewhere,....er," I said, trying to think of everything I knew about Great Leighs off the top of my head. "It's not too far off the centre mark on the map."

"Yeah? I think we should try there next then. I get the name Great Leighs."

Extinguishing the candles we had one final walk around the churchyard trying to do a bit of unsuccessful ghost watching.

We tried Great Leighs church first. Anne shook her head as we looked up at the beautiful round tower of St Mary's. "No this doesn't look right." We conducted another quick meditation, perhaps we could at least find out if we were in the right area.

"We have to go down," stated Anne positively. "It's very low. I see us all with muddy boots and we have to go down very low, like underground. They've conducted their ritual low down somewhere and I can still see them putting this large sword into the ground. Then they go across two fields to a church or ruin."

This sounded most bemusing. It could mean all sorts of things; an underground chamber, maybe a crypt or tunnel, or maybe it was just a hollow in the ground, perhaps even it was just somewhere at the bottom of a steep hill.

"Could it be Anne, that the place isn't low but it's surrounded by banks of earth so it seems it?" I questioned.

"Yeah.....maybe," said Anne doubtfully. "Why can you think of somewhere."

Duncan and I went on to explain that while driving down the A130 from Dunmow to Chelmsford we had passed a few miles from Pleshey Castle which we had visited on a few occasions before. We had both commented that we hoped it hadn't been their point of call as it has always had such a lovely atmosphere.

Anne didn't sense any water at the site and we knew Pleshey to be surrounded by a filled moat. If the site was Pleshey she would probably have known there was water near by but it was the best option we could think of, so we noted it as a place to visit that evening. First however, as we were in the area, we thought we would check Little Leighs church just to be sure so we could eliminate it from our list of possibilities, such as it was.

Noting the dedication was another St Mary the Virgin (she's a very popular lady) we entered the churchyard. Straight away Anne stated this wasn't the place. The church was locked as it was being fumigated, so rather than linger and waste time, we continued on our way to Pleshey.

It was threatening to rain as we pulled up to park on the road near to where the footpath begins. The castle is a large earthwork which is the remains of a Norman motte and bailey. It has been said of Pleshey that, 'It ranks as one of the great defensive sites of medieval England, a place of major civic and military importance in it's heyday.' There is a bridge over the moat which is unique in Britain. It has a single arch and is one of the oldest brick bridges in Europe, probably dating from the fifteenth century but possibly older. The whole of Pleshey is surrounded by earthworks, the outer bank of which is possibly pre-roman in origin. The village once earned the name of Tumblestoun due to all the earthworks.

Pleshey Castle is privately owned and in the care of a firm of Estate agents based in Chelmsford, Strutt and Parker, but it is clear that it is visited by a few people as the fence to the side of the gate is very easy to climb. Although on occasion we do enter private sites which is strictly speaking trespass, we never cause any damage to a site or leave litter. Part of Pleshey Castle's beauty is that because it is privately owned, only those really interested make the effort to go and see it. So mostly it is totally untouched (except by sheep), therefore the atmosphere has been interfered with less and even non-psychics like myself can sense it is a special site with memories still stored there and not yet eroded away by the passing of a lot of people. Having negotiated the fence we blundered our way around the steep slopes in the dark.

"Well we're getting muddy boots, so that's right," commented Anne sliding down the bank. Why we didn't all walk around the side with a shallow incline I don't know. We worked our way down until we were at the moat's edge, the lowest point we could reach. We were all laughing and joking about how wet it was underfoot, when another incident happened which sent us all into fits of laughter (far too like toilet humour to deserve a full explanation here, but very funny).

"I don't think this can be the place, not with us all laughing like this," commented Duncan.

"No, we don't usually manage to enjoy ourselves this much at the places they've been to, do we?" added Anne, wiping tears from her eyes. She went on to explain, after we'd all managed to get a bit more serious, that the site felt like it could be possible because of the low feeling to it but it just felt far too clean and happy. Just to be sure we retreated to higher and less damp ground to conduct a quick meditation, the results of which just confirmed what we already thought. Both Big Jason and Duncan could see a green haze of sparkling light just as if it had already been cleaned but this was probably the castle's natural energy.

We left Pleshey that night pleased they hadn't desecrated a beautiful site but still no closer to the centre.

* * * * * * *

It was a fortnight later on Wednesday, 16 November, when we could next all meet to resume our search. We met outside Jason D's house in Chelmsford and deciding that the road was an inappropriate place for a meditation, we chose to go to Galleywood churchyard, on the outskirts of Chelmsford, for some peace and quiet away from town.

Getting out of the cars, Anne (who had driven over with Richard and Big Jason) came over to Jason D, Cally, Duncan and I. "I had a dream a few nights ago. I was just telling Richard and Jason about it in the car. It was about another group, doing the same thing as our lot, only they were in Kent. They had a similar lay out of a web but they're definitely a different group. Then I saw them all working together and combining under one head man." If what Anne had seen was true, it appeared we were now looking at a far larger picture than we had originally thought.

Still discussing the matter, we walked towards the church armed with maps galore and a determined frame of mind as we all hoped that tonight we would have success. In the calm of the churchyard we all once again tried to focus our minds on the location of the centre of the web and once again we were all grateful to Anne as she was the only person to pick up anything. The rest of us with our comparatively meagre psychic ability failing us dismally.

Anne described what she could see. "Well, much the same as before really. They're in this very low place that I've said about before and they're performing a ritual there with this sword in the ground, then they finish and go up across 2 fields; it's very bleak. I then see them approaching a building, maybe a church but I can only see one wall and that's blank. They go up a hill to the building and I can see them with a burning cross. They then scatter the ashes from it all around the churchyard." It was a vivid description but unfortunately still gave us very little to go on with regards to the location.

Back to the maps. We knew we were now looking for somewhere that was bleak with a church on a hill or rise and had a very low point near by. I suggested Great Canfield as another possible spot, none of us had ever been there before but I knew there was a motte and bailey castle near to the church and it was very close to the exact geographical centre of the web. I reasoned that Anne had said Pleshey's motte and bailey had the right 'low' feeling to it so perhaps Great Canfield was similar, it was worth a go. While we were over in that direction, Richard also suggested we visit a church he knew of just off the A120 between Dunmow and Takely. This was he said very bleak and had a strange ambience to it.

Here we go again we thought, as we returned to the cars all checking the petrol gauges just in case.

Once at St Mary's, Great Canfield we noted on the map that the motte and bailey, which like Pleshey is probably of Norman origin, was at the back of the churchyard. Anne's expression didn't look hopeful right from our entering the churchyard. There were too many houses near by and even if the motte and bailey did have a low point as she'd described (which didn't look likely) you wouldn't have to cross a field to get from it to the church. We all decided we would like to return there in the daylight as it looked like an interesting place and we knew of some points of interest in the church itself such as a thirteenth century wall painting of the virgin and child and a carving possibly representing Odin. However, this wasn't our intended final destination for tonight.

All Saints, the next church we visited at Canfield End, however, looked more hopeful. It was set in a expanse of open fields with no houses near as Anne had described but here there was no low point or hill to go up to the church. It felt possible for the 'circle' to have visited there though because the atmosphere was very dark, none of us felt comfortable. We were all feeling thwarted at our lack of success and considered possible reasons for this frustrating situation. Was there a centre site at all or had Anne been mistaken? I didn't think so. To come so far on a quest so accurately it seemed highly unlikely that Anne would have made such a huge mistake all along in her conviction that this crucial point exists. Besides it seemed logical to have a centre point into which they could draw all the energy which they had collected towards. Also to make 13 points means to keep the symbolism of the sacred number. Our discussions continued; maybe they had cloaked their central site behind a 'wall' as they had Castle Hedingham and maybe we should repeat the meditation which we had carried out at Coggeshall church to break through it. In this conversation it came up that perhaps that was what they wanted us to do and we would fall into some kind of trap they had set. In my mind I suddenly saw that the centre site was an egg and if we broke into it a mass of tiny spiders would stream out all over the countryside. I got a shiver up my spine as a result of my over-active imagination and tried to change the subject.

We all felt once again we were getting nowhere fast and had for the time being run out of suggestions. Aggravated and frustrated we decided to call it a night and went for a drink in the Queen Victoria in Dunmow, to discuss the matter further.

Over the course of our search for the centre numerous suggestions had been made; Beauchamp Roding church for its magical potency, but the lay of the land seemed to be wrong. Felsted burial ground, but this has no building as Anne had seen. Leez priory remains seemed very promising but is on very private property. A Saxon burial ground in Broomfield, Chelmsford sounded good until I was told it is now a bit of waste ground behind some houses. The Dene holes near Grays were suggested and maybe the spiders web would be in the shape of that of a funnel web spider, so the central site would be outside the main ring. We discounted this possibility when Richard explained to Anne that the sides of the holes are very steep and you need ropes to climb down into them. Anne felt sure she would know if we would need to go to those lengths to get into this point in the ground which she could see. We also thought Grays would be stretching the distance a little too far. It appeared we were running out of choices, we would have to change our thinking and look for another way to locate this enigmatic centre.

Chapter Fifteen

SPIRIT OF THE ROCK

At the final meeting of Earthquest (which was temporarily disbanded on 7 November) Anne told us about some poltergeist activity she had been having in her house for a couple of weeks. Things were going missing and she could sense a black presence in her bedroom. As time went on she began to feel sure this was connected in some way to the quest and that they had sent it to her to perhaps prevent her from finding their central site. This presence had been in Anne's house for approximately 4 weeks when it was decided that enough was enough; it clearly wasn't going to go away of it's own accord so we ought to try and get rid of it. On Sunday, 20 November, we all gathered at Anne's house in Hockley. We were joined on this occasion by John and Kerry Horrigan (some other members of Earthquest). They had more experience at 'ghost-busting' than the rest of us and besides, we thought it might be a good laugh. We enjoyed the afternoon chatting and having a guided tour of Anne and Brian's collection of around 50 snakes. Eventually, Anne, Richard, John, Kerry, Duncan and myself all went up to Anne's bedroom to see if the 'being' was around and find out what it was and what we could do about it. We thought that if, as Anne said, it had been sent by the 'circle' to prevent her from finding the centre then it would know the location of the central site. We would have to work out a way to trick it into telling us.

None of us quite knew what to do so we thought we would play it by ear. We ascertained from Anne that it was present in the room. She could see the black form of a head, torso and arms, hovering in the corner. She described it as not good or evil, just amoral. After I had accidentally sat right on the spot where Anne could see it we settled down. Gathering round a candle in the darkened room we carried out a meditation. There were a few minutes of silence before Anne spoke up, "He says he's Syphilis." Oh no, not this again we all thought. Silence followed again, so having received no further information we paused to study some books. In a book on mythology we found the answer to why Anne had, for the second time, picked up this unusual name.

"Does Sisyphus sound like the name you've got Anne?" Richard questioned.

"Yes that's it! Not Syphilis, Sisyphus." We had it. Sisyphus was a figure from Greek mythology, a hero of Corinth sent into the underworld. Perhaps we thought the answer to finding the centre lay in the rhyme Anne picked up at East Hanningfield on our third visit there.

Cast the Runes
Play the cards
Sisyphus be here
Sisyphus beware

Maybe we had to cast runes or play cards with it to get our answers. Well we didn't have any runes so that wasn't possible but Anne had a pack of playing cards which she went and found. We would see what would happen if we played the cards with him.

"How many cards do we have each then Anne?" questioned John.

Anne paused a few seconds before replying. "He says seven each." John dealt out seven cards to each of us and an extra pile for Sisyphus, the resident entity.

"What next?" asked John having finished dealing. We all sat looking bemused thinking how bizarre this scenario was turning out to be. Anne meanwhile had gone quiet again and was staring at the spot where she could see the black figure.

"He says we've got to see who's got the highest."

We all turned our cards over and examined them for anything which may have meaning. John had the King of Spades and Kerry had the Queen, which we thought strange considering our opposing group were working with the suit of Spades. Stranger still was that Anne had the Jack of Spades the character which she had identified right from the start as the person who's job it was to retrieve the artifacts once their work was complete. This of course was exactly what Anne was doing, only hopefully getting there before the full desecration had taken place. The rest of us had nothing notable in our hands at all. Sisyphus' hand however had 2 Aces in it. It had won, which wasn't quite what we had intended. We all rapidly decided that perhaps playing cards with it hadn't been such a good idea. If he was going to win then we weren't about to get any closer to finding the central site from him.

Changing tactics we returned to the mythology books to gain some more information about this character. Sisyphus was a King of Corinth and committed a treacherous act against Zeus whilst making a bargain with Asopos, the river god, whom he had asked to provide a spring for his people. Zeus wouldn't let this treachery go unpunished and sent the daemon of Death to claim Sisyphus. However, Sisyphus didn't yield to death and instead bound the daemon with strong chains. As punishment for cheating death he was sent to Tartaros, a region of the Greek underworld set aside for those who anger the Gods. Here Sisyphus was set the eternal task of rolling a great boulder up a hill, where upon it rolls back down and he has to again push it back up to the summit.

"You haven't picked up any stones recently have you Anne?" asked Duncan suddenly. Knowing how Anne likes to collect small mementos of sites he had suddenly thought that perhaps she may have added a stone to her collection.

"Well yes I have actually," said Anne standing up and walking over to a small table. Lifting the cloth covering the table she pulled out a fairly sizable lump of rock, what could be described as a small boulder. "Brian and I found it at Kits Coty in Kent. We got talking to a local and he told us that a farmer called Mr Green had blown up the west end of the long barrow with dynamite and that you could still find bits of the stone scattered over the field. So we looked and found this. I just knew it was part of the original barrow. I know I probably shouldn't have taken it but you know how I like to collect things."

"How long ago was this then?" questioned Duncan.

"Oh about," Anne paused as the relationship between this rock and Sisyphus dawned on her, "four or five weeks ago." We all smiled as we realised we had found the key to getting the answer we wanted. It seemed that the poltergeist activity and black figure had all started as soon as Anne and Brian had bought this rock home with them and that both the rock and entity were in the same room. It seemed we now had a way to bargain with this entity. We had his rock and therefore his connection with this world.

It appeared this connection between Sisyphus, the rock found at Kits Coty in Kent and Anne also had a wider implication. Anne had already stated that she felt the group we were trailing had a sister group working in Kent. Kits Coty is a major ancient site in Kent, so if such a group were

Above: The rock we took to calling the Sisyphus Stone.

Below: Kits Coty dolmen in Kent, where Anne found the stone.

working on a network similar to that in Essex it seemed highly probable that Kits Coty would be part of such a network. It also seemed far too coincidental that the same deity had been picked up at an Essex site involved with this quest and in connection with this stone from a site in Kent. What appeared to have happened was that on an innocent walk through the Kent countryside Anne had unknowingly stumbled on part of the Kent group's activities, who were using the same mythical figure as their Essex counterparts. Because of Anne's knowledge of the Essex group she must have subconsciously picked up the stone imbued with an imprint from the Kent groups ritual.

John now mentioned that earlier, while meditating he had seen a church on a raised mound and picked up the name, 'Cwm.....something' as in a Welsh name. Knowing that the church he had seen wasn't in Essex (such churches are short in number there) he decided not to mention it until now. Now it seemed John's vision may have been relevant as our discussion continued. Perhaps he had seen a Welsh site (hence the name) and maybe this was a site on a similar web in Wales. It was all complete conjecture but it looked interesting and provided us with a bit more food for thought.

The Kent connection certainly points to the possibility that at least 2 groups are working together. Is there a possibility there are more involved, could we perhaps be looking at a national network, we questioned? With the hint from John it certainly looked like we would have to bear the possibility in mind.

Turning our attentions back to the job in hand we concentrated on Sisyphus again. Just to be sure he was securely bound to the rock, as he is in mythology, we conducted a creative visualisation exercise. In a medative state we all saw unbreakable chains come from a yoke around his neck and bind themselves to the rock. This we knew would ensure that wherever the rock went he went too and that he couldn't escape.

"Right now we can get down to business," said John having thought of a way to get the information we needed out of the entity. "Tell it Anne, that we want to know the location of the centre site." John then held the stone over the candle flame.

Anne sat still, staring at the spot where Sisyphus appears. Suddenly she exclaimed, "Great Leighs! He's burning!" John hurriedly took the rock away from the flame as it was clear that Anne was picking up very strongly on Sisyphus' emotions. She was panting hard and looked quite shocked and drained. It had worked though, we now had a definite place name. We had already visited Great Leighs but perhaps we had just been to the wrong spot or at the wrong time. We would have to make a return visit.

Anne had quickly recovered and was quite unaware of what she had said. We filled her in and proceeded to discuss the situation. Now we had the answer we required from Sisyphus we had to decide what to do with it and its rock. We talked about banishing him so Anne could get some sleep at night again without his unwanted presence disturbing her. Some daft suggestion arose like microwaving it. What exactly does happen if you microwave a haunted stone? We also thought of dropping the rock into a river and the running water would then dispel its magic. But what if we needed to use it again to tell us more information? For the time being we thought we'll put it outside in the garden, then decide what to do with it later.

We all stood up and carried the stone out to the garden.

"Ha, is there no end to our cruelty," proclaimed Duncan in a over-dramatic villainous tone, "we've deprived it of central heating."

Anne returned to her bedroom just to check and reported back that it felt a lot better, he was definitely gone from there.

It had been a bizarre evening but we now had an answer to the location of the central site and a greek mythological figure chained to a rock in the back garden!

CHAPTER SIXTEEN

THE ELUSIVE THIRTEENTH

Even though we now had a definite place-name for the central site we were all quite despondent regarding the quest because we had been led such a merry dance towards the middle of the web. Great Leighs was as much as we knew, so we yet had to work out where exactly in or around the village was the spot where they had carried out their ritual desecration. My uncle, Michael Grafton lives in Great Leighs so I asked him if he knew of any likely spots where a dark coven may go to carry out rituals. As I expected he looked at me as though I was mad but knowing about my strange hobbies he didn't mock. Michael suggested we have a look at an area over towards another village called Fairsted. He said how he and his wife Debbie had been out walking one day and had chatted to a man metal detecting in a field near 'The Square and Compasses' at Fairsted. He told them Fairsted had been built on the site of a Saxon settlement. Michael then drew me a map to describe the lay of the land between that field and the back of Great Leighs church, marking on a footpath and river. It looked quite promising, you would have to rise up a hill from Fairsted and cross over fields to approach the church.

We next all met at St Anne's Castle on the Braintree to Chelmsford road, reputedly the oldest Inn in England, on Wednesday 30 November. Our first topic of conversation was of our encounter with Sisyphus and Anne gratefully extolled to us how wonderful it was to be sleeping soundly again since the stone had been ousted to the back garden. This seemed like proof enough that we had been successful. We also discussed what we had heard from John. He had phoned Anne to tell her about a dream he had had one night. He described an aerial view of England, like a map, and it was marked with all the places in the country where there were similar web networks. As often happens with dreams he couldn't remember the exact names or positions when he awoke but he got the feeling of there being four areas. Was this further proof of a wider view of things? We all felt time would tell.

Turning back to the here and now I told the others of my uncle's suggestion and deciding it was as good a place to start as any we set off to check it out.

We parked at the pub in Fairsted and quickly found the footpath my uncle had described; it turned out to be the Essex Way. A path which not surprisingly runs over the whole of Essex. Armed with torches we set off for an evening walk. Luckily there was a bright moon so we could clearly see the lay of the land and spot Great Leighs church tower about a mile away over the fields.

"How does it feel Anne?" I questioned, as we walked along. "Do you reckon we're on the right track."

"Yeah, I feel like I'm getting close." Anne's face looked positive, she could definitely sense we were in the right area.

We followed the path along until we came out on to the road.

"What's that?" said Richard, pointing over to the trees towards the church. There was a light flickering between the trees. Following the beacon we found it was only a fire lit in the midst of an avenue of trees to burn off brush wood but it had drawn us closer to the church and Anne was growing more positive by the minute that we were so close to the central site. It had to be the church.

With bell ringing practice booming out, we entered the churchyard and followed the path round to the back. Anne walked over to a small but steep slope at the east end of the church and walked down it. She then headed to the fence before she turned to look back towards the church.

She nodded, "Yeah, this is definitely it. Look this is the hill they came up and that's the wall I saw," she said pointing the features out. From where Anne was standing all you could see of the church was this one wall, all the rest of the building including the tower was obscured. "I can see them all walking up the slope with a burning cross and scattering the ash all around." The sharp rise up was as she had described in her vision only we had all misread it to be a hill. The field beyond the churchyard was barren and bleak as she had described. We hadn't visited this far corner on our previous visit to this church. This may have been the reason why Anne didn't identify the site the first time or perhaps we had just been too early and there were no warning hints of their intentions to desecrate the site as there had been at Much Hadham. Also we had had help from Brigit on Ring

The sharp rise leading up to the East end of Danbury church which Anne had seen psychically.

Hill to aid us in finding Much Hadham prior to their visit. We just didn't know why we hadn't decided that this was the place the first time round, but we'd found it at last now, and that was all that mattered. Next all we had to do was find the hollow in the ground or underground spot where Anne had seen the ritual taking place.

Off over the fields we set and under Anne's direction headed for the far side. Here we turned and wandered down along the field boundary. We were all thrilled to have at last found this elusive centre site but looking at the lay of the land we didn't hold out much hope of finding the low point of the ritual. The field was flat and barren and had no distinctive features at all. Anne was quite bemused that we couldn't find this place she had seen; she obviously still felt we were very close. We came to the small river, the Ter which runs alongside the church and paused by the riverbank. Here there was a patch of dry ground at the level of the river under a large spreading tree. It looked just right; it was lower than the surrounding land and would have given the appearance of being underground by the tree spreading out over it. Maybe it was the place, maybe it wasn't, we couldn't be sure. Anne had no strong feeling on the matter and we all felt sure that if the low point had been near water Anne would have picked up on the presence of water nearby; being one of the four basic elements it is a strong influence on a psychic.

Once again, all we could do was agree to return in the daylight so we might be able to see the next field over in case they had come from further away. We gave the churchyard a quick proviso cleansing on a psychic level which would help until we could return later to finish the job off properly. We felt some form of stronger cleansing than simply creative visualisation would probably be in order. The spreading of the ash around the churchyard would have been a strong influence and would be hard to dispel. An artefact is a single object which can be easily removed (if you can find it) but ash would need to be washed or blown away to totally dissipate it.

* * * * * * *

It was unfortunately left far too long before we could return to Great Leighs. I'll make no excuses, this is a true story and the truth is that we simply didn't get around to it. Some of our group were still very despondent about the quest and doubted we would be able to find the place of the ritual. There just looked to be nowhere like Anne had described in the vicinity. It was discussed that perhaps what Anne had seen was symbolic and perhaps they had only thought themselves underground when they performed the ritual so that is how Anne had seen them psychically. This was certainly a possibility but we had to make a return visit in the daylight just so we could totally rule out the likelihood of there actually begin a physical underground or low spot.

Having got Christmas over with, the few outings which were organised were all unfortunately postponed due to illness, work commitments, other quests etc. We eventually arranged a definite date for 4 February 1995. Just Anne, Duncan and myself remained for this concluding visit. Anne had arrived early and had already wandered around the churchyard before Duncan and I pulled up. She told us she had instantly felt a pull to the left hand side of the churchyard (the north side). It was left at that for now and we set off, accompanied by our new puppy, Miggins, over the fields.

We started by following the same line across the fields which we had previously taken in the dark, and then continued on over another field towards a small patch of woodland. It didn't look hopeful. We checked the woods for any dips in the ground, but there were none. Standing back to examine the lay of the land Duncan suggested we head down into the valley again. It was the only low lying point around, it seemed the only option. As we walked down the field we came to a hedgerow which began in the middle of the field, separating just a small section of field from the rest. In the hedgerow was a small stream with a spring at its head (hence starting in the middle of the field). We had had huge amounts of rain recently and the water was flowing quickly, towards the river.

"Oh, it feels funny here," commented Anne, "something's definitely not right here." We continued to walk down a short way. I too could sense that the atmosphere was peculiar just along this strip of hedge.

"Can you hear voices?" Anne questioned. Duncan and I both shook our heads.

"Is it the bubbling of the water you can hear?"

Anne shook her head, "No it's definitely voices, like mumbling. What's that? It's coming from there," said Anne pointing through the hedge to a small mound on the other side.

"I don't know," replied Duncan, "a fallen tree stump maybe. Let's go and have a look." We crossed the ditch further down over a small bridge and headed back up to the shape we had seen.

What we were greeted with was *a small underground chamber* containing an old pumping system. Most of it was sunken into the ground with only a small mound put over the roof above ground level. It clearly hadn't been used for some years. Duncan descended down the steep steps

Anne and Duncan examine the underground chamber over the fields from Danbury church. Was this dismal little pumphouse potentially the site used by the magical group?

to investigate further. The room was about 5 feet square and 7 feet high, with a small amount of water lying in puddles on the floor. Was this dismal little derelict chamber where Anne had seen ritual magic take place? It seemed highly unlikely, but there was a certain amount of pointers to suggest that perhaps it was. Firstly we had felt the atmosphere change on approaching the area and it was in direct line from the church over the two fields as Anne had said. Also it was completely underground, despite the fact we had more or less given up all hope of ever finding such a place. The pumphouse was in a fairly ruinous condition which is perhaps what Anne had sensed when she mentioned a ruin when first looking for this central site, also all the information about an underground chamber had been revealed by Anne on out first visit to Gt Leighs. Finally Anne completely refused to go in it, despite the fact that she is a far from squeamish lady and only the weekend before had quite happily gone into a crypt as part of another quest. It certainly seemed like we had found the site of the ritual despite its totally unglamourous appearance.

The only major inconsistencies which we could think of were that Anne had said the whole group had been there for the final ritual and yet to fit 13 people into the little room would be very tight to say the least. She also hadn't sensed water and this spot was right next to a spring and finally she had no overwhelming feeling that 'this was it'. We spent some time discussing the situation and trying to reason out what actually could have happened on the night of the ritual. Having returned to the far side of the hedge we again commented on how the atmosphere seemed worse on this side of the hedge and stream than on the side with the small shelter. Ideas began to form and we reconstructed the following scenario as our solution as to the events of the night.

We believe they chose the spot on the far side of the hedgerow to carry out the main bulk of their ritual as it is a small sheltered corner of the field, not visible from any roads or houses. Here all 13 of them had gathered and ritually planted a sword in the ground as part of the process of bringing their completed web into its final stage. Being in the open air when it came to lighting their cross they perhaps had difficulty or maybe part of the ritual required being underground and so one or a small amount of the group resorted to the shelter of the small pumphouse. It may have been necessary in their rites for them all to be present at this moment but obviously in the confined space that wasn't possible, so they used a creative visualisation exercise to picture themselves all in the little chamber at the lighting of the cross. This would have led Anne to see them on a psychic level all present at this moment whether they were actually there or not. They then left the chamber once the cross was burning and started their journey over the fields towards the churchyard. The spring we reasoned may only be seasonal and only due to the exceptional amount of rain we'd received was it flowing now, so perhaps it was dry when they carried out the ritual; hence Anne didn't sense water.

It was all fitting together. The passage of time had weakened the affects of their magic so making it hard to tell instantly if this was the site or not, but reasoning it through had, we felt, led us to an acceptable answer. This sequence of events as we understood them once again brought total reality and practicality into an almost fantasy like scene.

Having agreed that this was undoubtedly the place we resolved to cleanse the small chamber with some incense. Duncan was just emerging from this task when a farmer came over the field towards us. 'Uh oh, now explain this one,' we all thought. We were only a short distance from the path and Anne's quick thinking saved us from the embarrassing situation of trying to explain why we were lighting up incense in a derelict old pumphouse.

"We've lost our dog," Anne shouted to him, as Miggins had conveniently disappeared into the hedgerow. "Miggins".

Right on cue Miggins emerged from the greenery. "Ah, here she is," Anne called, and with that the farmer raised his hand in farewell and turned to go back to the footpath before he'd even got close to us. It looked like having a dog along with us questing would prove useful from now on.

The North side of Gt. Leighs church where our final actions against the web were completed.

Having cleaned the little chamber we followed in our opposing groups footsteps back towards the church. Anne then explained that she felt they had taken the ashes of the cross and sprinkled them all to the north side of the church. It was that side which mainly needed cleansing. We firstly set incense at the small bridge which you have to cross to approach the church from the back. They must have had to have crossed it and would therefore have probably brought with them any streams of negative energy from the ritual site. Setting the incense on either side would hopefully disrupt these flows and dissipate them away. We then completed both a creative visualisation cleansing ritual and sprinkled some holy water around the affected area to totally eradicate the last vestiges of the effects of any corrupt magic.

As I have said, questing is a real life pursuit and therefore often the unexpected or disappointing happens; this is the nature of the beast. Although their grand finale had proved to be a dingy little shelter, hardly the underground chamber we had been hoping to find, we were still very happy just to have found it because we had nearly convinced ourselves that we never would. All too many quests never have a satisfactory conclusion so to simply be able to say we had successfully completed our quest against the web was very satisfying indeed.

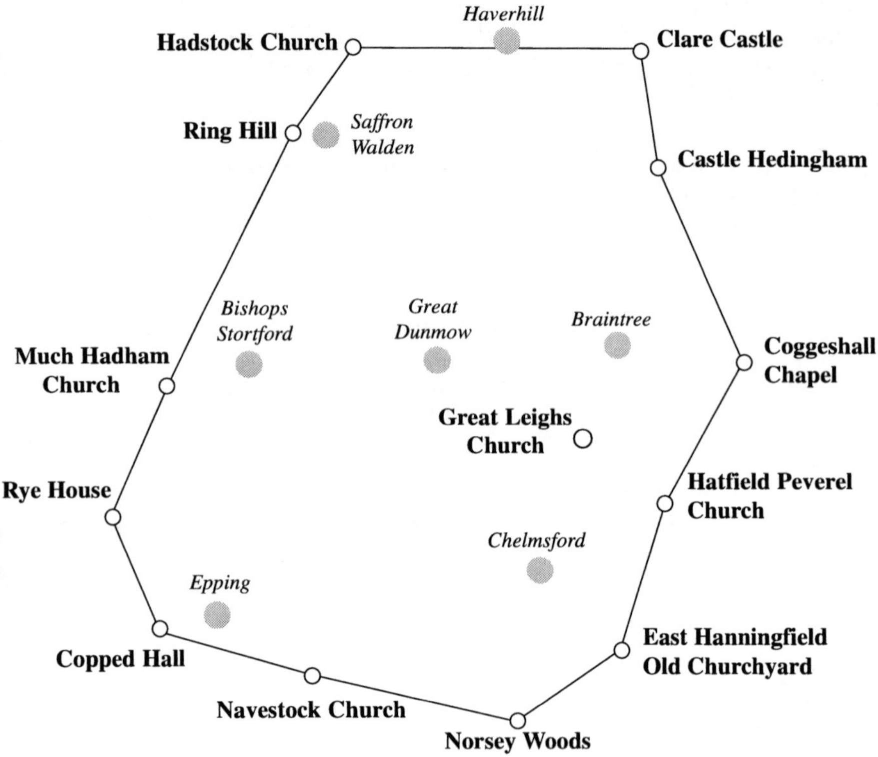

The layout of the completed web.

CHAPTER SEVENTEEN

SISYPHUS RETURNED

After a time it was decided by Anne that the 'Sisyphus stone' should be returned to Kits Coty. The presence attached to the stone was not inherently evil in itself, however Anne still found it disturbing. We decided to make a day of it, so a trip was arranged down to Kits Coty for some of the members of Earthquest who had stayed in touch and now met at fortnightly meetings in Chelmsford. On Sunday 5 March we all met in a car park at Aylesford, Kent and headed off in convoy up the steep hill to where the top of the footpath to the dolmen meets the road.

The remains of Kits Coty long barrow now consist of a sizable dolmen (three large upright stones supporting a large capstone) which was once the eastern end chamber of the barrow. This is set in a large field which commands a beautiful view out over the valley below.

Having all taken in our fill of the stones and their surrounding field, which still has a slight rise in it of the original long barrow, we got down to our intended business. We had discussed the situation previously and had decided we would take the opportunity of having a 'haunted' stone in our possession to see if we could try and photograph the 'spirit' connected to it. For this we would all have to concentrate on the entity bound to the stone and see it as a real figure ('a greek bloke' as John described him). We all gathered around the stone which we had placed on the ground at the western end of the barrow remains. John took the lead for this meditation so once everyone was ready and cigarettes had been extinguished he began. First having taken us all through a breathing exercise he led us all to seeing this 'greek bloke'. He then went on to re-affirm the chains connecting him to his rock. Finally the meditation was left open for comment from any impressions received be anyone.

Duncan spoke up first, “I think we’re supposed to give him the task of re-building the barrow.”

John paused for thought and obviously deciding this was a good idea proceeded. “Right, see him rolling a boulder up the hill and in doing this he’s re-building Kits Coty barrow. See the barrow gradually begin to take on form as it would have appeared about 4,000 years ago when it was built.”

While our group of meditators lingered on this imagery Anne was meanwhile seeing something quite different.

“He’s putting the chains around mine and Big Jason’s ankles,” she said in a somewhat disturbed tone.

“OK, picture light burning away these chains and returning them to binding Sisyphus to the rock. Everyone, see it as strongly as you can, it’s very important that he stays with this stone.” This exercise seemed to work as everyone went silent.

After a few more minutes with no further information being offered up John brought the meditation to a close. We unfortunately hadn’t discovered if Sisyphus had been part of another similar web in Kent or exactly what his original purpose at the barrow site had been, but we had succeeded in giving him a new and beneficial task. If Kits Coty had been a site in a Kent web the trail may well, like at Great Leighs, have now become too cold to be clearly discerned by a psychic. However, if any budding psychic in that area of Kent is feeling active I strongly recommend Kits Coty as a good place to start, and would be very interested to hear of any developments.

As for our attempts at spirit photography they failed dismally. There was a moment after the meditation when Anne could very clearly see a face on the stone and tried to take some photos of it herself. Her camera jammed repeatedly and although both John and another friend of ours Matthew Devine from Sevenoaks, who are both very competent photographers, tried to fix it, it seemed like it wasn’t going to be fixed. When Anne got home she had another go, just on the off chance, and her camera worked perfectly! It certainly seemed like Sisyphus was camera shy as although two other camera were pointed at the stone at around the same time nothing unusual was to be seen in the prints (one of which is shown earlier: see Ghost-busting).

CONCLUSION

In conclusion to the 'Essex Web' and it's makers we are still not fully aware of exactly what they were up to. There seemed to be no pattern other than geographical to the sites chosen. There wasn't any preference towards hill-tops, water related sites, churches, a certain period in history, etc. They also seem to have no magical basis or related properties connected to them, eg. all of a masculine or feminine aspect. It seems they were entirely chosen for their geographical positions. However, there must have been a site they specifically wanted to include in the south-westerly corner of their web, hence the diversion from the pattern. This must have been the Gatehouse at Rye House or Copped Hall. I suspect the latter as it is clearly a powerhouse of occult activity. However, with all the others it seemed that they had been chosen purely for the fact that they were the nearest place with a strong enough energy field for their purposes. As all ancient and sacred places have this quality it left the Queen of Spades and her acolytes choosing from churches, castles, hill forts and other monuments of a symbolic or historical nature. It is our opinion that this group under cover of darkness tainted their chosen sites with their corrupted rituals and negatively charged artifacts, leaving a trail of spiritually devoid places.

Why they carried out this series of rituals can only be guessed at. They desecrated the sites they visited and used, but whether this was the direct purpose I doubt. I expect that the disruption and corruption of the energies was a side effect of the rituals and effects of the markers they left behind. The markers, their attempts to repress spring and their fixation with the death symbolism of the Spades all must have served the purpose of drawing together energy for some reason in that area. I can only repeat Anne's suggestion of people in high and powerful places using it to further their own ends. Weaving their own destiny by corrupting the energy of sites into the form of a web.

However, they were foiled in this task. Our band of questers broke their malignant web and baffled their effect on the environment and atmosphere, and with our removal of their artifacts erased of their dirty etheric footprints.

There will never be an end to black quests, as their will always be opposite forces working against one another; that is the way the world works, and the way another quest will begin.

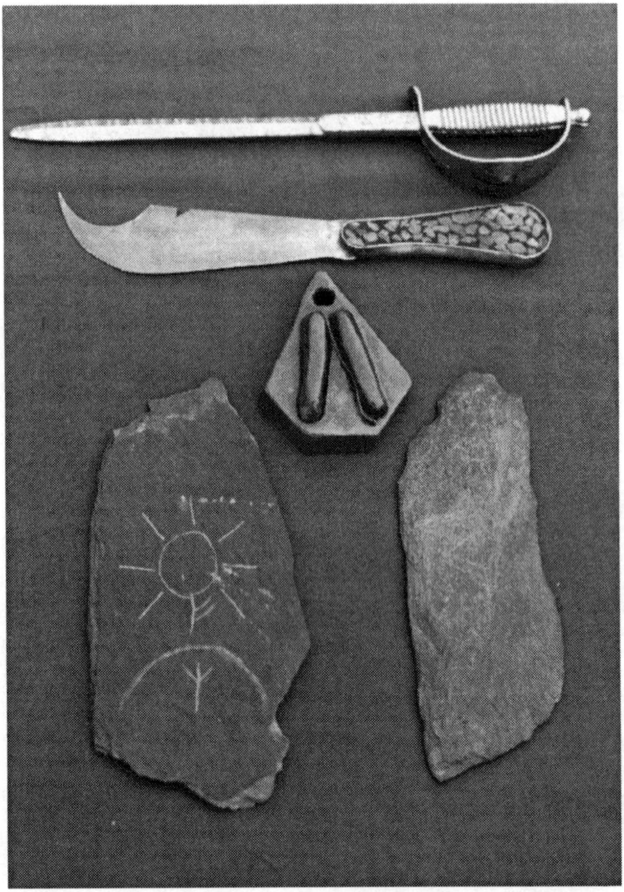

YOUR TURN?

If you and maybe a group of friends have an interest in ancient and sacred sites and you think either yourself or a friend may be harbouring a psychic talent then get out into the landscape and see what happens. The most important thing is that you all get on well and trust one another. It's also good if everyone is willing to try and gain information, even if, like me you feel you are as psychic as a plank. You never know when you may get the odd snippet of information or an odd feeling and the more you try and develop your psychic ability the more likely you are to have success.

In this book I have outlined most of the basic procedures of questing, such as they are, and the protection methods are briefly described in the Appendix. These along with your own moral values and common sense are all you need to know to go questing. It helps to have some knowledge of earth mysteries, basic magical principles, ancient sites, religions, mythologies etc. but what you need to know largely depends on the subject of the quest, and what you don't know then you can try and find out.

The research side of things plays a large part in some quests (probably even more than the psychic's information on the more historical quests) so some competent researchers in your group can be a major advantage. Try and record your quests for future reference, important things all too quickly get forgotten so it's advisable to take a pen and paper or a dictaphone along with you. Other bits and bobs which you may need are; local maps, a compass, torches (and spare batteries), warm clothes and sensible footwear. Optional extras for your questing kit which we've found useful include; dowsing rods or a pendulum, incense, a camera and holy water and/or salt for cleansing purposes. Finally, and most important, don't forget your sense of humour, and if things go from the daft to the ridiculous just go with the flow.

Appendix

We used various methods of meditation and protection along the way. The meditations we use are all forms of creative visualisation. This is basically using the power of the imagination to achieve results on a magical level. If you see something strongly enough in your mind and believe that it will work you will be able to affect the energies around you. It is the belief in this form of meditation that I think is most important to its success. All our group believe in it and are comfortable with the method and therefore it seems to be very effective. Some meditations we do consist of just standing in a circle and remaining silent while in a relaxed state. While in this state your mind is open to the influences of the subtle energies present at a site and so we wait to see if any images or impressions come to mind. Others may involve speaking out loud during the meditations if any information is received. This enables everyone to focus their mind on that same things, so strengthening the imagery and allowing others in the group to tune in to the same image or guardian spirit to perhaps gain more information. The third main form of meditation we use normally involves someone in the group, (usually Richard) actually talking us through the beginning of the meditation. This leads us in mind all to the same place or along the same line of thought, thus concentrating all our minds on the same imagery at the same time. This strengthens the connection with the information and answers we're trying to receive at the time. Once we have reached a place or summoned a guardian we then fall silent to each centre our minds on the job in hand.

While in a medative state you may be vulnerable to unwanted influences so when going deep into meditation it is advisable to use some form of protection. There are two main forms we use depending on our requirement at the time. The cone of power is the protection we use during meditation. This has many purposes for not only does it protect you from unwanted forces but also acts as an enhancement for meditation taking you deeper into a relaxed state than just standing at ease. It is similar to flicking a switch in your head, when you start to build the cone of power your brain gets to know to how shut off and begin to wind down. It also can be used as a vehicle to travel in mind and spirit to another place. The cone itself is built by first seeing a small pin-point of light form in the centre of the circle. This then begins to move round, spiralling out until behind you and gradually get faster and faster and bigger and bigger and so leaving a streaming tail behind it like a comet. Having formed a ring around you this acts as the base of a wall of light which you picture spiralling up around and over you. Once over your head it comes together to form a cone or beehive shape, this is your basic cone of power. You can then picture the light swirling underneath you and then filling the interior of the shape you have formed to provide added protection. You can include many other extras in this meditation such as breathing and aura boosting exercises if you wish. The main point to remember with the cone of power is that once raised it must be dismantled when you have finished with it. To not do so is like leaving etheric litter behind you.

The other main form of protection we use is the Cabbalistic cross taken from the Cabbala. This protection is best for walking into a situation where you may be likely to come under psychic attack and has saved us from ill affects on many occasions. Rather than remaining linked to the ground like the cone of power this is anchored to you so moves where you do.

There are many ways to build the Cabbalistic cross. The method we employ goes as follows. The group form a circle and each raise two fingers skyward. You then see a point of white light forming way up in the sky and moving downwards, this comes towards your fingers leaving a column of white light up in the sky. You use this light to draw the energy across you to form a protective cross, anchoring it at your head with the word ATEH, then your chest with the word MALKUTH, at your right shoulder saying the words VE GEBURAH, then you left shoulder with the words VE GEDULAH and finally with your hands clasped in front of you over your chest say LE OLAHM, AMEN while imagining the light forming an all encompassing cross within you, going right down to the ground, getting brighter and stronger. Once completed picture the column of light returning back to the tiny speck in the distance up in the sky. This you can then walk around with knowing it will be the first line of defence should any unwanted influence try and draw your energy.

BIBLIOGRAPHY

AUSTON, E, *Coggeshall in History and Legend,* Friday House, Coggeshall, date unknown.

BORD, Janet and Colin, *Ancient Mysteries of Britain,* Diamond Books, 1986.

BIRCH, Mel, *Historic East Anglia in Camera,* Images Publication, 1988.

CASSIDY, Raymond, *Copped Hall - A Short History,* Waltham Abbey Historical Society, 1983.

CASSIDY, Raymond, *Copped Hall in its Heyday,* Waltham Abbey Historical Society,1986.

CIRLOT, J E, *A Dictionary of Symbols,* Routledge and Kegan Paul, 1973.

COOPE, D Jason, *Using The Runes*, Aquarian Press, 1986.

COOPER, J C, *An Illustrated Encyclopaedia of Traditional Symbols,* Thames & Hudson, 1978.

GRAVES, Robert (introdution by), *New Larousse Encyclopedia of Mythology,* Hamlyn Publishing, 1959.

HOUGH, John, *Essex Churhes*, Boydell Press, 1983.

JONES, Arthur, *The Shire County Guide To Hertfordshire,* Shire Publishing, 1988.

MILLER, Hamish and **BROADHURST**, Paul, *The Sun and The Serpent,* Pendragon Press, 1989.

MURRAY, Alexanders, *Who's Who in Mythology*, Bracken Books 1994.

NEALE, Kenneth, *Essex Heritage,* Leopard's Head Press, 1992.

PENNICK, Nigel, *The Secret Lore of Runes and Other Ancient Alphabets,* Rider, 1991.

PEWSEY, Stephen and **BROOKS**, Andrew, *East Saxon Heritage - An Essex Gazetteer*, Alan Sutton, 1993.

PUSEY, Richard, *A Discovery of Old Essex*, Robert Hale, 1985.

PUSEY, Richard, *Essex - Rich and Strange,* Robert Hale, 1987.

RODWELL, Warwick, *Under Hadstock Church,* Circle Services, 1974.

THOMAS, Nicholas, *Guide To Prehistoric England,* Book Club Associates, 1960.

TYSON, Donald, *Rune Magic*, Lewellyn Publications, 1992.

INDEX